Zei

Zen Stories

The Irreverent and Sacred Teaching Stories of Lee Lozowick

Edited and with Commentary by
Sylvan Incao

Third Eye

ZEN STORIES

First Indian Edition 2004

ISBN 81-86505-70-9

This Edition published in arrangement with the
Hohm Press
Prescott, AZ 86302, USA

by THIRD EYE

An Imprint of
BHAVANA BOOKS & PRINTS
101, AVG Bhawan, M-3, Connaught Circus,
New Delhi-110001 (India)
Phones: 011-23415198, 23415205
Fax: 011-51517091
e-mail: rajanarya@vsnl.com

Printed by Elegant Printers, New Delhi
This editon is for sale in Indian sub-continent only

CONTENTS

PREFACE

In the spring of 1994 I was attending a small college in northern Arizona. I wasn't quite sure why I ended up there, as I was no longer interested in the subject that I had once applied for, and was now studying religion, philosophy and human development. For the past few years I had devoured every new angle on spirituality that I could get my hands on. These resources had fed me, inspired me, and pushed me forward for some time. But, by the end of my second year in college, I was beginning to feel that something big was missing in my life. It became increasingly difficult to find the same inspiration and guidance from this material that I had lived by for the past several years. My personal practice began to collapse, and moods of despair and depression swept over me daily as I struggled to figure out what I felt, believed in or thought I knew.

I tried studying the known traditions, but did not resonate with them, finding them dry, distant. Meanwhile, my inner world continued to collapse. Secretly I dreamt of being born a thousand or two thousand years ago when the great masters and sages walked the earth—alive, real, accessible, and surrounded by disciples. The world around me looked horrifyingly hopeless, speeding forward recklessly in an irreversible superficiality.

I would ride my bicycle around town, through the dimly lit streets and back alleyways at night, searching for some café, some bookstore, *someplace* in which I could ease the groundlessness and discomfort that plagued me.

About that time I first caught the drift of a certain teacher named Lee who lived in the area with his community. I didn't pay it much attention—I wasn't interested in communities anyway, although plenty of my friends were. But the indicators persisted and the clues grew stronger, strong enough that they began to tug on me, to get my attention. It seemed that this teacher was a spiritual teacher, even called a master by many of his students. I didn't really believe this at first, but I kept my ears open. The thought of a spiritual master living in the suburbs was absurd to me. Besides, this was the twentieth century. Spiritual masters were a thing of the past. As far as I was concerned, all that remained today were books about such persons.

Underneath my skepticism, however, I felt a surge of excitement, almost exhilaration. I pressed my friends and acquaintances for more information. Who was this teacher? What was he all about? What did he teach? Only one man seemed to know anything. He informed me that this teacher sang in a rock'n'roll band, called *liars, gods and beggars*, that performed locally, and invited me to attend a gig one Saturday night in an old historic warehouse on the north end of town.

Conspiring with some friends, and very unsure of what I would find, I went out to the warehouse that night. The parking lot was dark and quiet, but the thump-thump of drums and the wailing of electric guitars coming from the building was unmistakable. Walking up to the front door, we hesitated; no one said anything. A momentary fear welled up in me. Then, we went in.

A large dance floor opened before us, with thirty or so dancers moving excitedly to the music. At the back of the room another fifteen to twenty people sat in chairs or stood talking and watching the band. I recognized nobody. The music blasted across the room at us with a force that seemed to stop our further entry into the building. I scanned the room, fixing my eyes on the small stage set up in a corner, where a six-piece all-male rock band was playing.

The members of the band looked to be about middle age, several were bearded, and most had long hair, either flying loose or gathered in a ponytail. All were dressed casually in jeans and t-shirts. To me they appeared like any ex-hippie rock band, talented but obscure. In the center of the stage a man with dark sunglasses and a bushy graying beard and hair was leaning into the microphone. His voice boomed in the awkward acoustics of the warehouse. It was throaty, gravelly, rough.

"That's the teacher," my friend yelled into my ear, pointing to the stage.

"The guy playing bass?" I yelled back. The bassist looked like the best bet—head shaved and looking rather stoic, cool.

"No, the guy singing."

I looked over again at the man hidden behind sunglasses in the center, who was now jumping up and down in front of the lead guitarist with a tambourine in one hand, the microphone in the other.

"He can't sing," another friend yelled over at us, a look of incredulity on his face.

The vocals *were* quite non-melodic—half-sung, half-spoken.

We stood and watched for some time as the band played song after song, unsure of what to make of this strange scene. I tried to discern the lyrics but the sound was too rough to really follow them. One thing came through, however—the lyrics didn't seem particularly "spiritual," and for that matter, neither did the man who was supposed to be the teacher, nor the band around him.

The picture before me presented a strange juxtaposition: no one was smoking; no one was drinking; and yet here were all these people dancing and gettin' down to the sounds of this full-on rock band, a band that was supposed to be headed by a "spiritual master." It didn't fit into any frame of reference that I had, nor match any experience I could relate it to.

As the night wore on I began to loosen up a bit and dance to some of the songs, still watching the lead singer-teacher out of the corner of my eye. In my mind I was trying to piece together everything I had heard, read and studied and believed about spiritual masters with what I saw before me—a bearded fifty-something, middle-class, sunglass-wearing Jewish man, half-singing half-yelling into the microphone, making jokes at the expense of the small audience gathered there, and cussing with all the crudity of a truck driver. *This* couldn't be a spiritual master. Spiritual masters are holy, sacred, wise beings, not bad rock'n'roll singers in back-alley warehouses in no-name towns.

But I couldn't easily dismiss the experience of that night. I couldn't resolve the discomfort I felt between what I'd been told and what I saw. I was unwilling to believe that I'd been lied to and yet unable to believe that this strange man was who people said he was.

In the coming months I attended more rock'n'roll gigs, using the time to carefully scrutinize this man called "teacher" and see if there was more to him than first met the eye. There was. But it took a closer investigation over the following months and years to begin to reveal what lay beneath the rock-singer façade and to understand that façade's place and importance in Lee's teaching work.

Since 1994 I have had the opportunity to travel with Lee to India, Europe, and various cities throughout the U.S., to witness first-hand the enigma of his public persona, whether on stage or giving a talk. Over the years, this *koan* has not resolved itself, but deepened, continuing to reflect back to me my own internal contradictions and struggles to understand beyond the level of mind. This book is not the culmination of such understanding, but a passing glimpse. Its true value lies in the transmission of the teaching through Lee Lozowick's "Zen trash," and is due completely to the storyteller of these tales.

INTRODUCTION

On all the spiritual paths and in all the religions of the world there has always been an oral tradition, a way in which men and women kept the great truths alive by speaking or singing them to one another, to their children . . . and to their children's children. The sacred teachings were thus preserved, often kept fresh and vital by the energy of the storyteller, teacher, or minstrel. They were also modified for the time and culture in which they were presented.

Besides carrying direct transmissions of doctrine, this oral tradition was generally ripe with myth, parable, poetry, song, and practical examples—teaching lessons that the masters of the way had made at one time. These elements often had a much stronger impact than all the scriptures, codes, laws and formal dogmas that comprised the bulk of the tradition. Consequently, the great stories were more likely remembered, whether or not one liked or ever applied the lessons they made.

In the Western world, for example, most people, regardless of their religious affiliation, are familiar with a few incidents from the life of Jesus—his spending forty days in the desert, or changing water into wine, or his Last Supper and crucifixion. With the historical Buddha, many people know the tale of his life as a prince, living in a palace, shielded from the harsh realities of life and death; or they have heard of him sitting under the bodhi tree, meditating until enlightenment came. These stories of the great ones bring the teaching and the tradition to life for us. They are more than mere historical referents. They may actually be genuine communications of the teaching itself, often recreating and thus invoking the mood, presence and essential view of each tradition, lineage or master that they speak of.

Jesus used parables as an integral part of his teaching method. He told of the good shepherd, the barren fig tree, the prodigal son. Such parables were simple stories, comparing a tenet of faith or practice to a commonplace example from the ordinary lives of the people of the time. Everyone in Jesus' audience would have known about shepherding; everyone would have been familiar with the native fig tree.

The Tibetan Buddhist tradition speaks of *termas*, which are relics and sacred texts that were disguised or hidden as a means of protecting them for future generations. Such *termas* are thought to be time-coded —remaining hidden until they are needed, and then discovered by designated and adept "treasure gatherers." Traditional teaching stories from all cultures are *termas* in a way. The meaning and potential for transmission that they hold and may be able to impart is not always immediately evident. Access to the wisdom of these stories depends upon the intention and ability of the practitioner or student of the path, who must search out this wisdom, study it—see it, feel it—and thus extract its levels of meaning from the matrix in which it is presented. And, such a matrix may be thick with the rough edges of the teaching's various disguises.

In Sufism, the humorous fables of the beloved fool Mulla Nasruddin demonstrated the stupidity of humanity's self-obsession in a way that all could recognize. The Sufi masters, like the wise teachers of the other traditions, knew that they had to find a device that would disrupt the usual sleepwalking state in which people generally wandered. They told stories. They made jokes. They offended their listeners—anything to keep them alert enough so that something of value could enter into the otherwise well-defended fortress created by the mind.

In the Zen Buddhist tradition, stories and *koans* have long been a vivid and essential part of the process of training the mind. *Koans* were, and are, designed not to reveal their meaning to the student instantly and easily, but to throw that student into a crisis of mind, a crisis so acute that the only resolve is to break through into a non-conceptual, direct apprehension of reality, known as *satori*. Such *satoris* often came only after years of struggling with a *koan*, trying to "understand" it. Such struggle was essential, however, as it produced in the student a kind of rawness, a fertile ground, in which the meaning of the *koan* could at last be revealed. Today, due to the popularization of Zen in the West, many people are familiar with ancient *koans* and teaching stories, such as: "A student goes to a Zen teacher and asks for the teaching. The master doesn't answer at once, but keeps pouring tea into the student's teacup until it overflows onto the table . . ."

Just because one may have heard this tale a dozen times, and can repeat it to others, doesn't mean that the lesson has been learned, however. Tossed about in casual conversation or considered in a hasty, light and entertaining fashion, one can easily assume that, because one glimpses the meaning conceptually, one has realized the meaning. A popular literary magazine recently depicted a cartoon of two monks—one old, one young—sitting in *zazen* posture. The old monk turns to the younger monk and says: "There is no 'What's next?'" We laugh, but who *really* gets it?

Entertainment was not and is not the essential purpose of a *koan* or a teaching story. Treating them facilely does not harm them (a traditional *koan* is pure, immutable), but may encourage losing sight of a deeper possibility, of a sacred, albeit challenging, opportunity to consider the story's true purpose. All the *koans* and traditional Zen teaching stories were originally given and passed down within a lineage, and as part of the training in a working spiritual school. They appeared within a context of practice, a context of *sadhana* on the path, in relationship to a teacher or master, and were meant to be considered within this context. Herein they bore the fruit they were designed to bear. Therein they were given the honor they deserved.

Then we come to *Zen Trash*—Lee Lozowick's renderings of centuries-old teaching stories, not just from the Zen tradition, but from others as well. As you begin to read the traditional teaching stories in this book you may question whether "doing them the honor they deserve" was thrown out the window, so to speak. That's when you begin to encounter Lee Lozowick. That's when the *koan* of this book begins to take effect.

The original Zen stories convey a kind of purity, of simplicity. As Lee put it, "The Buddhist stories are always very nice because they eliminate all of the messy details. The teacher just makes a gesture and the student gets enlightened. It's clean and it's crisp and it takes no time. It's all very neat." But Lee's *Zen Trash* stories aren't—nice and neat, that is. Out of the several hundred renderings that were found in transcripts from Lee's seminars and talks over the past two decades, those that he told in a more conventional manner didn't meet his standards for this book. "No 'straight' stories," was Lee's immediate directive to me as I began this project.

Despite the many twists and turns that Lee has introduced into these old tales, giving them a contemporary punch, their communication is essentially the same as it has always been. As Thomas Cleary writes in *Zen Antics:* "The real purpose of Zen stories is not in documenting events of the past, but in their effect on the reader, and so this is their real history."(*Zen Antics, 100 Stories of Enlightenment*, Boston: Shambhala, 1993, p. xiii) The stories in *Zen Trash* are bound to the same purpose.

The stories that follow *are* messy—full of digressions, changed endings, colorful new details—not because Lee thought it would be cute and fun to put his own spin on the story, with his own unique flair, nor because he is just being irreverent to be bratty. But, as the Sufi master or the Zen teacher might do, these stories are presented to confound attempts to "understand" them intellectually, thus stirring up an altogether different possibility.

These stories are, in Lee's own words, "trash," in much the way a street-wise musician might use that word—like the way "bad" has come to mean "cool" or "good," and "shit" has come to mean all one's prized possessions. The dictionary defines "trash" as that which is discarded; as rubbish; but also as foolish or pointless talk; as nonsense. Yet, as can be learned from the enigmatic presentations of other traditions and cultures, it is often in the utterances of fools that the greatest wisdom can be found.

Lee Lozowick's teaching is not an independent entity, but rather a part of a tradition and a lineage. He has directed a practicing spiritual school for over twenty-five years. His stories, then, are best used and appreciated in the context of a serious approach to the path, although they themselves will often appear far from serious. In fact, they are highly entertaining and amusing, and if you are not offended, disgusted, or disturbed, you will certainly laugh a lot.

Lee's "trash" might serve you only after several readings. It will be worth the effort. If his stories entertain, be entertained. If they provoke and shock, be provoked and shocked. If they move you to question and consider, then question and consider, and don't be easily satisfied with the first answer you get. Allow these stories, or even one word or line in these stories, to take root in your being. Because, although in form these stories are just "trash," in essence they hold what every traditional teaching story has always held, the possibility of glimpsing reality. But they won't give up their secrets easily. It's going to take some time.

So, says lee,
you want God?
You want blisses?
You want relationship?
What is it worth to you then?
Is it worth your health,
your peace of mind,
your equanimity?
Is it worth your sanity?

If you want to imagine God,
you may get away with it very
inexpensively—only act like
your mind is untroubled,
act like its "all one" and suffering is an illusic
But if you want to meet the Creature face
to Face, ah, sighs lee
you must be prepared to be
misunderstood by your intimates,
ostracized by your friends,
shunned by the worldly.
Yet how ridiculous to even elude
to what you must be prepared
for—no preparation is the only preparatio
All of this babble. Is it poetry? No, it's
trash—throw it out—forget lee said
it—forget you read it.
Do you think you understand? Have you
swum on the moon? Have you watched
your own birth? Has the sun burnt
you to a well-roasted crisp?
Do you think you will be full of wisdom
if you realize God? You will be a
drunken fool, a pauper, a twisted man.

Of course you still say you want God.
Then have Him if you wish.
lee mourns you then, and celebrates you now.

—Lee Lozowick, December 1982
(*Death of a Dishonest Man, Poems and Prayers to Yogi Ramsuratkumar*, Prescott, Ariz.: Hohm Press, 1998, pp. 215-216)

The Koan of Lee Lozowick

Lee Lozowick is an enigma in today's spiritual "scene." Whether in Arizona, Europe, Canada, Mexico or India, his life might appear as a blur of activity—touring and performing with his Blues band until all hours of the night, giving public talks and seminars week after week in Europe, Canada or Mexico, and infrequently in the U.S., and minding to several ashrams and a growing body of students on several continents. His speaking style doesn't fit the picture that many people have of what a spiritual teacher is supposed to sound like. His approach can be rambling and highly provocative, yet at the same time rich with transmission of the dharma. Lee once described himself as a "five-foot eight-inch American enema," a literal laxative—to those interested in his medicine—for one's cultural, social and habitual constipation of ideas, expectations, projections and fantasies about spiritual life and practice in the company of a master.

The stories in this book were excerpted from public talks and seminars of the last twenty-five years. Sometimes they popped out in seeming discord with the flow of the subject being spoken about, or the question being asked. Lee might interrupt an apparently serious exchange by recounting one of these tales, or by telling a series of jokes; or he might digress for half an hour into seemingly irrelevant matters—speaking of an Arnold Swartzenegger movie, for example—only to pick up the thread of the original subject when the audience has been laughing for a while, or loosened up in some way. At other times, these stories flowed seamlessly out of a point Lee was making, driving it home with unmistakable clarity. And then, as quickly as it had appeared, his irreverent story might disappear again into a clear stream of dharma, leaving the mind to paw at the empty air in attempts to make sense of it all.

Two traditions meet and weave together what makes up the style and focus of Lee Lozowick's teaching. One is the Baul tradition, and the other is the path of crazy wisdom. The Bauls of Bengal in northern India are a 700-year-old sect. Their way is characterized by a blend of pure devotional Vaishnava Hinduism and tantric Sahajiya Buddhism, with strong resonance to the mystical Sufi path. The Vaishnavites take their name from Vishnu, one of the three great gods of the Hindu pantheon. Their tradition is steeped with devotional expression, particularly to Lord Krishna, one of the primary incarnations of Vishnu. The Sahajiya path—literally "natural" or "easy"—expresses "a system of worship in which the natural qualities of the senses are used, not denied or suppressed"—a fundamental description of tantric practice. (Edward C. Dimock, *The Place of the Hidden Moon*, Chicago: University of Chicago Press, 1966, p. 35)

The Baul synthesis is characterized by four primary elements: there is no written scripture—their teachings are given through song and dance; God is believed to be found in and through the body, thus their emphasis on "sadhana of the body," or *kaya* sadhana; the use of sexual and breath energy for sadhana; and the tenet of absolute obedience to a guru or master.

Perhaps the most notable characteristic of the Bauls is that they are wanderers, beggars, and musician-poets, praising God in song, dance, and mystical poetry. For the Bauls, their teaching is encoded in their songs and poetry, and is accessible through the appreciation and study of these forms. As wanderers and beggars they are looked down upon in India, considered vagrants in polite society and heretics among the traditional religions. Their religious life is not bound by orthodoxy or convention, but arises from an instinctual and lived relationship to the divine. The Bauls' daily life evidences a passionate and yet profound reliance upon the Beloved, or personal God within, and a celebration of that relationship in all its ecstasy and its heartbreak.

Lee Lozowick teaches in what he refers to as the Western Baul Tradition. The form differs somewhat from that of his Eastern Baul predecessors—the teaching *does* appear in written form, and the music he writes and performs is Blues or rock'n'roll rather than mystical poetry—but the essence of relationship to the Divine Beloved remains the same. Like his Eastern counterparts, Lee draws from several traditions in his work, feeding his students from the wisdom of both East and West. In one teaching session he might share Zen stories, read from an eminent master of Tibetan Buddhism, quote the Christian mystics, and talk at length about the principles of the Fourth Way as exemplified by George Gurdjieff.

Lee is also somewhat of a heretic in the spiritual scene, recognized and respected by some, avoided or disparaged by others. He is well-known for his directness, his fluency with street language, his down-to-earth sense of humor, and for his unwillingness to compromise by catering to demands of seekers in the contemporary spiritual marketplace. The participants in his seminars are often shocked to learn that they won't spend a weekend doing anything they are used to experiencing in other workshops—no coupling up, no group exercises, no massage, no rolling around "feeling" the teaching in their body. Instead, they will simply sit, perhaps ask questions, and listen, for six or eight hours a day. "Dharma sesshins," his students have come to call these weekends.

In 1976 Lee met a beggar in Tiruvannamalai, southern India. His name was Yogi Ramsuratkumar. Although he was dressed in rags and continually referred to himself as "this dirty beggar," Lee soon came to recognize how great this unassuming yogi was, and that he was, in fact, Lee's guru. Shortly after this meeting Lee began to write and send Yogi Ramsuratkumar poem after poem, proclaiming his praise of the Beggar King. These were poems of heartbreak, of devotion, in which Lee repeatedly asked for madness, the kind of divine madness that Yogi Ramsuratkumar embodied. Over the next twenty-five years, more than one thousand such poems flowed from Lee to Yogi Ramsuratkumar, capturing and often revealing the essence of Lee's relationship to his spiritual father. These poems, like the mystical poetry and songs in the Eastern Baul tradition, hold and convey not just the devotion of Lee to his guru, but the communication and transmission of the teaching, a literal "road map" for his students to decipher and follow.

Crazy wisdom, the other thread in this weave of Lee Lozowick's approach, is a way of teaching that has appeared in almost every spiritual tradition of the world, and for thousands of years. The term "crazy wisdom" seems to be a recent invention, but encompasses a vast array of expressions from the Native American trickster, coyote figure, or heyoka, to the Fools for Christ of the Middle Ages, within the Christian tradition. Georg Feuerstein writes in depth on crazy-wise teaching in his book, *Holy Madness: The Shock Tactics and Radical Teachings of Crazy-Wise Adepts, Holy Fools and Rascal Gurus* (New York: Paragon House, 1991).

> From the conventional point of view, the crazy-wise teachers are eccentrics who use their eccentricity to communicate an alternative vision to that which governs ordinary life. They are masters of inversion, proficient breakers of taboos, and lovers of surprise, contradiction, and ambiguity. They share these skills and penchants with the traditional figures of the trickster and the clown. (p. 3)

Crazy wisdom or "holy madness" does indeed seem crazy to the rational mind and common sense morals of most people, but that is exactly because it is designed to confront, shock, and otherwise confuse that very rational mind. Such behavior and teaching turns us upside down, giving an entirely new perspective to our ordinary view of life, including and especially our spiritual life. The crazy-wise teacher is willing to employ a broad range of tactics and appearances in the service of bringing the student to a greater realization of the teaching (or Reality), including but not limited to provocation, insult, humor, crudity, and the use of sex, alcohol, and money in unconventional and often socially unaccepted ways.

Of course, such methods and behaviors create reaction and conflict even in those committed to a path under such a teacher, not to mention the general public, and call into question all kinds of issues of trust and the abuse of position and power. As there are plenty of false gurus roaming the circuit, purporting to be realized and very definitely abusing the adulation and resources given them, such questions *are* important, although, perhaps, not relevant to a public forum, as the average person doesn't have the foundation or the objectivity to consider such subject matter in any way except conventionally. But, serious seekers will certainly be called upon to deal with such apparent contradictions for themselves. Challenging the norm on this matter, Lee suggests an even more radical perspective:

> It's a very interesting thing about Japan. All of the responsibility lies with the student. The Zen roshis . . . they could fuck sheep, to be blunt. They could be drunkards, they could be heroin addicts, they can do anything they damn please. And the way the Japanese look at it is, if someone is stupid enough to become a student of a roshi that's obviously an asshole—well, they deserve it!
>
> We've got it backwards. We put all the responsibility with the teacher, which doesn't require the students, who are supposed to be the ones who are learning something, to learn anything!

The presence of charlatans passing themselves off as crazy-wise gurus does not invalidate the presence and value of genuine masters, whose appearance may be exactly the same, in form. In essence, for those who have the ability to sense, feel or read at this level, or have the patience to learn such discrimination, there is a vast difference between the charlatan dramatizing unconventional means and the genuine crazy-wise teacher. The former, though he or she may even appear to be serving students, is responding to the dictates and needs of his or her own "spiritualized" ego, to self-importance, and to the desire for power and comfort. Such people are certainly fooling themselves, thinking themselves to be as awakened as they promote themselves to be, or as their followers advertise them.

The genuine crazy-wisdom teacher will act only in response to the needs of his students and to those before him, regardless of his own comfort or personal preference, and will show up only in alignment with the context of the teaching. His or her only concern is the work of awakening students from a state of sleep or unconsciousness to a state of clarity, of seeing reality, and in moving such students forward in their maturity on the path. The crazy-wise teacher doesn't think up, plan or strategize their behavior, he or she is simply transparent to the transmission coming through them, responding to the needs of those who seek that transmission.

In the Baul path, the typical greeting and farewell is the enthusiastic exclamation: "Jai Guru!" which literally means, "Victory to the Guru!" "If the guru is victorious," Lee said during one talk, "the guru makes no profit; only the disciple makes profit. If the guru is victorious, it means the disciple becomes free, even free of the guru. But when the disciple comes to the guru as a baby, with no resources, no bank account, first the guru has to fill the disciple's bank account. The guru has to carry the disciple."

Such "carrying" of a disciple may not look good, especially in the light of modern demands for independence and the belief in equality for all. Nonetheless, the guru is willing to do it and to be misjudged for it; to be scorned, even, for the employing of non-conventional methods in the service of his function. No wonder the world calls such wisdom "crazy."

It is up to the serious practitioner or seeker to see through the show that the teacher may be presenting; to see behind the veils that he or she may be wearing. A little-known secret about the crazy-wise teacher is that, if he is genuine, he will always reveal himself, always let a little glance or a word slip that will give him away; something that will blow his cover. If we are paying attention we will see it, know it, hear it, sense it. There is always a hole in the curtain, and we are always being invited to peek through. Sometimes that hole will be obvious, sometimes more difficult to find. But it is always there.

An Evening With Lee Lozowick

On any given night in Frankfurt, Paris, or Mexico City, Lee Lozowick might be scheduled to give a public talk. The room would likely be simple or even bare, brightly lit, clean, unceremonious. In the rear, or to one side, several tables would be set up: a large selection of books in several languages, by Lee and other authors whom he supports, would be arrayed, together with CDs, tapes, t-shirts and anything else related to the work of his present musical ventures, plus, most recently, a selection of Indian bronzes. This is "The Sacred Bazaar," as Lee has taken to calling his traveling store. "Next year I'll be bringing soap and toothpaste," he might joke later in the evening, as he loudly and enthusiastically urges his listeners to "Buy my books!" throughout his presentation.

At exactly the hour that the talk is scheduled to begin, the man who has been standing behind the heavily-laden book tables will leave his post in another's care and walk to the front of the room, seating himself without explanation on whatever chair or pillow has been provided for the presenter of the evening. *The shopkeeper turns out to be the guest of honor!* Not quite what one might have expected from a spiritual teacher. But, as the evening wears on, there will be many more aspects of Lee Lozowick's demeanor and teaching style that won't quite match the general expectations for what a "spiritual master" is supposed to look or act like.

His appearance is often a shock to the unprepared. Penetrating blue eyes, gray hair knotted into thick, beaded dreadlocks, Lee is usually dressed in sweat pants and a t-shirt, with bare feet or simple sandals, regardless of the weather.

Over the years that I have traveled and studied with Lee, I have observed his intentional use of whatever physical elements occur in any space as ways to challenge, if not provoke, his audience. If the room is too hot or too cold, he will generally leave it exactly as it is. If anyone asks for a change of temperature to suit their comfort, he will most likely refuse. If there are not enough chairs, he will ask people to squeeze in tighter or sit on the floor. If we have trouble seeing him or hearing him, it will be up to us to adjust, as he will rarely change his position or the volume of his voice just to make things easier. These small discomforts alone will often be enough to drive out the most casual of curiosity seekers. As Lee's topic on any given night will almost certainly be about the possibility of transformation—from self-obsession to God-life, surrender, or genuine service—these simple inconveniences will provide his listeners with abundant fuel for self-observation, if they care to use them, generating the kind of internal "heat" necessary to accomplish any shift of consciousness. The alchemy of the evening will by now be well underway.

Alchemy, a word that describes an ancient process of transformation or transmutation, was the attempt to transform base metals into gold. The medieval alchemists first set up an appropriate chamber in which the process of transmutation could take place. This was also referred to as the "athanor," an Old English word for "oven." The chamber *had* to be an oven because the next essential ingredient to the process of transmutation was heat, a lot of heat. Finally, they needed "the philosopher's stone" or elixir—the ingredient that catalyzed the transformation of the base material into gold. This was the element that the alchemist sought for the longest, as it was the hardest to find. The catalyst was the key.

Whether literal gold was actually any alchemist's goal is questionable—the entire process of alchemy may have been a metaphor used to describe an esoteric process of a much higher order. The real base material was the individual human being: unconscious, habitual, conditioned by culture and society, filled with the impulses of survival, control, defense, reaction, and the longing for comfort. The transmutation of the unconscious creature called "man" into a truly alive and awake human being would mark the success of this more esoteric alchemical process. This type of transmutation seems to be the only one that interests Lee Lozowick.

His style of speaking—whether it is fast, rambling, coarse, provocative, eloquent, seemingly irrational and confusing, or pristinely articulate and clear—is often a source of confrontation, if not irritation, to his listeners. His words have been known to hit people in the head, the heart and the gut, all at the same time. What he talks about—whether it is sex, money, food, movies, the Bauls, his master Yogi Ramsuratkumar, the stupidity of TV, the need for surrender to God, his own life experiences rendered in a self-deprecating manner—is sometimes entertaining, sometimes disturbing. And this uncensored portrayal of who he is, what he is dedicated to, and how he relates to life will most likely evict the next group of seekers within the first thirty minutes. Perhaps Lee has just confessed that he would like to see the young blonde woman in the back row naked, or that all he cares about is selling his books and that he wants you to buy as many as you can afford—more than you can afford, in fact. Maybe he is insulting the audience with remarks about how mechanical they are, how predictable. Or maybe, if it is France, he is putting down Rimbaud or Verlaine. In one public talk in Belgium of 150 people, Lee mentioned how he believed Belgian chocolate was inferior to Swiss or French chocolate. Seventy-five people promptly walked out. For them, that simple scratch at their identification with their culture was too much. Their interest in what was behind the provocation was not strong enough to keep them there.

While some audiences will cheer Lee on, remaining in rapt attention to the end of his remarks and participating actively with questions for an hour or more, at other times the group will have dwindled to less than half its original size by the time of his conclusion. The experience they are undergoing is the "heat of the chamber" without which transformation of any type would not be possible.

Lee seems to monitor the heat very exactingly, in any number of ways, like providing ample room for laughter when things get too intense or serious. That is the alchemist's job: to maintain a balance among all the elements in the experiment—providing neither too much heat nor too little.

As the evening gains momentum, and the alchemical process—much like a truck careening along a narrow mountain road at full speed—begins to take effect, several other ingredients come into play. No matter who his audience is, because they are human they all come cautious, defended, wary or naïve in various ways. On an essential level, a participant may intuit that what is being offered is of lasting value. He or she *wants* to be transformed. But on a practical level she is suspicious, or critical, or perhaps the opposite—not critical enough, but blindly willing to believe the first thing someone says. Whatever our habit, it needs to be shaken up a bit, jostled loose from its post of protection where it's been crystallizing for years, perhaps decades. Lee's job, then, is a bit like a gardener's—he has to break up the hard dry surface of the soil before he can throw down some seeds. Humor and provocation serve in that loosening up or jostling process.

"So, this Amish couple is driving along one day . . ." he may begin, launching into a lengthy sexual joke, and then roll off three or four other jokes without pausing for the next ten minutes. Only then, perhaps, will he introduce himself. People will laugh or be offended, or both. But what the intelligence of the alchemical process knows is that ego can't keep up its guard as easily when it is laughing or when it is upset, disturbed or offended. The "feeling center" (Gurdjieff's term) will have been engaged, and even one's best intentions to objectively analyze and coolly scrutinize the situation—about who this man is and what he is saying—may be temporarily thwarted. People describe a sense of being thrown off balance by Lee's antics. The balance they have come to count on in their lives and in their world is, for a moment, out of their control.

As the evening progresses, those who remain in the room long enough, particularly if they are paying attention, might notice that the mood takes a turn at some point. Perhaps Lee has turned softer, more serious. Whereas earlier he may have answered questions with humorous or casual remarks, now he may be answering them very personably, gently. At last, it seems, an opening has been created into which a genuine consideration of the dharma can flow. Many of his favorite stories reflect a similar dynamic—like that of the great Tibetan master, Marpa, who, after all his selfish and grandiose gestures have failed, finally collapses at the feet of his teacher, Naropa, at a loss for what to say or do; ready, finally, to receive the master's teaching.

And so, sometimes after an hour or more of pummeling or playing with the audience, Lee taps the vulnerability he is looking for. Now the alchemist can begin the work of refining his approach to each person. The outer coarsest layer of psychological resistance to the ideas of the teaching may have been cleared away, if only momentarily, and the finer work of sculpting the base material of each one's humanness can begin. This is not to say that Lee will animate only seriousness and no more humor, bawdiness, or provocation. That flavor of Lee's communication will usually remain throughout every public talk. But, even that will have a different feel to it. He may still hammer away at his audience's projections, illusions or expectations, but he'll scale down to a smaller hammer, taking lighter, more precise taps than he did in the beginning.

Each talk is a new alchemical mix. While all the same principles for enacting the experiment may apply, the base material—the people present—will always be different. So the actions of the master alchemist will be different every time, too. Lee is unpredictable, always spontaneous. His movements in the room, his intonation, his words, the mood and style with which he is speaking, can be viewed as a specific and exacting response to the needs of those present, to the needs of the alchemy of the chamber. While he has developed a huge bag of tricks, otherwise known as "skillful means," over the nearly thirty years of his teaching work, by his own admission his work with people is completely instinctual, a result of his surrender to his master, Yogi Ramsuratkumar.

The spiritual teacher is much like a magician. The magician is up in front of the crowd, and he's talking non-stop. So, immediately, the brain is concentrating on trying to follow him, trying to understand him. Then he is promising to show you a trick, and telling you about it at the same time. But while he is doing his trick, he's waving his other hand, or blowing up a balloon, or shaking your hand, and before you know it, you've been had. The trick is done. How did he do that?

The magician, like the teacher of skillful means, knows how the mind works. He knows that if he is going to pull off his trick, he's got to get the critical analyzing mind out of the way, and that feat for him is relatively simple. A mere wave of the hand, some light gossip, a joke, a shiny wand, and mind is "had," seduced away by some passing flash.

The teacher's "trick" is to get the dharma out of the bag and into your pocket before you know what happened. And pretty much anything goes that serves this purpose. So, here is Lee Lozowick in front of the room—perhaps acting like a clown, laughing and inviting us to laugh, telling stories, insulting us, being fierce, arrogant, charming or entertaining—because he knows that, as far as ego is concerned, no amount of sincerity, devotion, commitment, or intention . . . absolutely nothing . . . will convince it to be dethroned. And ego's being dethroned is what *will* happen if the master has his way. So, like the magician, the master knows he has to trick ego—trick it into listening, into accepting the game, into going along with what the heart is yearning for.

> I'll tell you a secret. The way I communicate the teaching is, I hang it out right in front of people's faces so clearly that nobody believes that's it. And the rest of it is all drama, and excitement and intrigue. —Lee Lozowick, Freiburg, Germany, 8/31/97

Lee will often capitulate to the audience's projections by reassuring everyone that what he says is only his "opinion," only what he has learned from so many years on the path, and that anyone is free to disagree with him. In fact, if we don't like what Lee is saying, we're invited to write him off, right then and there. Lee will sometimes make people feel like equals, like peers on the path. And, of course, he will tell lots of entertaining stories. Whatever it takes to create an opening, to get mind off guard, to loosen up the armor of psyche that encases us, he will do!

But, beneath the external show, something else is happening. Transmission is the force of Truth entering our bodies, our beings, viscerally, literally. It is the essential form of the teaching moving from master to student beneath all the show, the antics, the stories, the words, beneath even the sincere and vulnerable exchanges, commitments, and relationships that are formed with the master. Transmission is the essential *raison d'être* of the master, and in Lee's case, the reason why he is willing to put himself out, again and again, to new people every day. All that we see, hear, or experience is set up to distract us, seduce us, entertain us into staying around long enough for transmission to occur. The dharma only becomes lived, embodied, real, in this way.

The possibility that even one person could be moved, affected, transformed in even the smallest way—as antithetical to appearances as this may seem at times—seems to be Lee Lozowick's intention. When questions are asked, for example, he will respond to them and turn the answer to the service of the whole group, if that is at all possible. Perhaps the questioner himself has no idea of what he is asking about, or is not even able to truly use the answer. That is of no importance if an answer would serve the larger group gathered. If anything can be of use, it is used. If not, it is declined, discarded. Maybe Lee will simply answer, "I don't know," and move on. Maybe it will seem that he doesn't even hear the question, responding to something else entirely, perhaps to the unconscious intent of the questioner, or to . . . who knows what!

In the midst of this flurry of activity, and throughout a typical evening, this "Zen trash" is thrown, like mercury added to the alchemical process. These stories often serve as a quickening agent in the experiment. They're exciting, entertaining, interesting—at least at first. And, because they are often rendered in such an iconoclastic and irreverent form, they cannot be easily dismissed or forgotten. Such stories are like poetry —they strike a different part of the brain, often circumventing the mind because they are not always linear or logical, and because they are more real to us than any theoretical explanation of dharmic principles. They are real because, as much as we may resist them, especially with the strange twist that Lee puts on them, they are ultimately about us—our lives and our lies, our struggles and our secret perversities, our dreams, our successes, our confusion, and our failures.

Favorite Themes

Despite his "street-smarts," his irreverence, and his engagement with rock'n'roll, the Blues, and other projects of contemporary relevance, Lee Lozowick refers to himself as conventional, conservative, traditional, even Victorian at times, and hard-line. We need only look at the themes he presents in his teaching work to see that he is not kidding.

Lee is an advocate of natural and ordinary life as the foundation for spiritual practice. He has reaffirmed constantly, in alignment with the principles of Baul sadhana, that God does not dwell in some day-glo heaven realm of the seeker's fantasy; but right here, right now, in the day-to-day challenges and tasks of our everyday lives. If people are touting their "spiritual experiences" or meditating their days away, running after their own "enlightenment," while their children or other family members are asking for their attention and help, such people are seriously confused. In his highly-acclaimed book, *The Alchemy of Love and Sex* (Prescott, Ariz.: Hohm Press, 1996), Lee wrote:

> Any kind of experience, no matter how ecstatic, that does not transform the experiencer into someone who essentially knows how to be with children, how to be with their family members, how to be with their mates in a loving, deeply caring way, how to be with all of life, is not God! Natural and ordinary life, the way it is, is the alchemical crucible—the space in which transformation happens. The Divine is not meant to be discovered in heaven. If the Divine was meant to be discovered in heaven, we would be in heaven and not here. (p. 5)

Lee talks a lot about men and women, and children, because relationship and sexuality are primary human concerns and functions. He fully endorses monogamous relationships, speaks in favor of the devotion and surrender of husbands to their wives, and wives to their husbands, and emphasizes the need to recognize and honor the real Feminine—in both men and women—in the world today. Based in his work of the last thirty years he has been honored as a child advocate. He is a staunch supporter of home-birthing, breastfeeding, natural medicine, holistic education (which may include homeschooling), and especially of the demand that adults model in their own lives what they ask of their children.

As a social commentator, Lee denounces the culture's dependence on and addiction to television, most computer technology, including e-mail, and many other supposed innovations of our times that have promised to simplify and personalize our lives, but which, in effect, have done exactly the opposite.

In the domain of spiritual life, first and foremost, Lee takes issue with all the watering-down of traditional spiritual practices and the many modern forms that have, in his opinion, compromised the great teachings. He is an ardent defender of rigorous practice, even extraordinary efforts in practice, and his stories and the heroes he emulates generally have to do with this theme.

Lee embodies the ideal of the master-disciple relationship as a primary means for the communication of the sacred teachings, no matter what religious tradition they show up in. Concomitant with this, he has taken an unwavering stand for the presence of the Master, or the Guru, or the Teacher, in the world, as well as for the traditional relationship of obedience and surrender that goes along with such an acknowledgement. And it is these positions that have earned him the respect of many and roused the indignation of many others. Ours is an age in which reference to the "guru within" or "the direct path" is used as the hallmark of sophistication and independence from antiquated forms. Yet, Lee holds firm in his commitment to awakening his students from the illusion of separation, based in his own realization that he is nothing, while his master, whom he affectionately calls his Father, Yogi Ramsuratkumar, is everything. "Only in knowing that one is nothing, however, can one realize that one is Everything," Lee has said.

How To Use This Book

As you read *Zen Trash*, the theme of making some form of payment for the teaching being given will be hinted at or directly explicated. It is another favorite theme that Lee will come back to, over and over. And it is a valuable one to have in mind as you begin to read this book.

Decidedly, you may already have paid something —the price of the book, or the trouble of borrowing it from someone else. You have set aside a half hour of your life, thus far, to engage what it has to offer. And, by so doing, you have entered into a reciprocal relationship of sorts with the author, whether you like it or not.

Whether that relationship will provide you with something of lasting value, however, will require that you ante-up further, and all along the way. But, let Lee throw some light on the situation . . . or some trash on the fire, as it were. Here's the first of it:

Naropa's story . . . it's a very long, interesting story. I won't tell the whole story, I'll just get to the point. He was trained to be a black magician and then he had many people killed, and then he felt bad about it—he had some remorse. So he decided he needed a teacher who could elevate him to the point where he could wipe out the bad karma from all the damage he had done as a magician. So he eventually heard about Tilopa, and everybody said, "There's no one like him. He's the guy for you."

Naropa sold everything that he had and collected gold, and went to Tilopa. So, he comes to Tilopa and he offers him the gold. And Tilopa says to Naropa, "Come with me."

And Naropa thinks, "Oh great, the master is going to give me some teachings." And they go to the lake and Tilopa takes the gold and throws it in the middle of the lake. This is everything that Naropa has . . . his entire life's treasure.

Understandably, Naropa gets a little upset. So Tilopa immediately squats, and pulls up his pants, and takes a shit on the ground. And as he shits, it turns to gold.

Naropa was suitably impressed, so he agreed to accept Tilopa's conditions as teacher, whatever they were.

This could have been about Naropa and Tilopa, or Marpa and Naropa, I don't remember. But anyway, you get the point, eh?

The master, by virtue of who he or she is, cannot give if there is no one there to receive. Nor can he give out of proportion to the recipient's need and ability to use what is given. The master is lawfully bound by the principle of reciprocity—he cannot pour tea into a full teacup, as the analogy goes.

Everything that comes from the master has to be invoked by the need of his or her surroundings; by the necessity of his students or of those present. Everything must be paid for—not necessarily with money, as Naropa did with bringing all his gold to Tilopa, but in some form, be it with time, attention, questioning and considering, devotion, commitment, work, service. Nothing can be given for free, despite the notion that "the best things in life are free," or that the truth should always be free. Actually, as Lee Lozowick will point out throughout the tales that follow, the exact opposite is true. What is "free" is habitual human life: eating, sleeping, sexing, growing old, and dying. On the other hand, genuine education, wisdom, maturity, integrity, dignity and elegance must be earned, learned, worked for, paid for. In the trades, a skill is not learned by seeing it done once. It is learned and mastered by applying discipline, patience and effort over years and years.

So, too, is the teaching earned, Lee will reiterate. Idle curiosity doesn't pay for much. Neither does mere interest, even sincere interest, nor spiritual materialism —the grasping accumulation of more and more methods and experiences—which actually drains our resources rather than replenishing them. The only thing that *really* pays for the teaching is work, struggle even, to invoke it. It *will* come forth, readily and with no other option, but for this to happen we must have "necessity" for it.

The master is like an invocation- or a dharma-dispensing machine, to be crude. He is packed with the complete line of the best brands of the teaching, but payment must go into the machine for the goods to come out. Whether we are physically present at a talk given by a master, or simply reading a book, the same law applies. If the questions we ask, internally or externally, or the demand we make upon ourselves in engaging the material is solely intellectual, based in mere curiosity or spiritual materialism, that is generally not enough payment for a deep answer. Most likely we will receive only a brief, evasive or humorous response, either directly or indirectly.

If there is a more pressing need in us, however—a driving desire to know the truth and to live it—then we may get a very different answer. We may find that the book in hand is totally different from the same book read from the point of view of curiosity. Knowing something about this principle of necessity, we can bring our intention to bear as we read. We can be more sensitive to when we are internally arguing for the sake of argument; whether we are wasting our valuable energy in agreement or disagreement with the writer's style or opinions instead of attuning to the impact that the subject is having on our whole body-mind complex. We can challenge ourselves to formulate a question that more accurately captures that real need. After a period of time, simply enduring the heat that a genuine, unanswered question will create, we may start to notice that the answers start appearing in the most unlikely places—in the piles of trash that we had previously overlooked or disdained—or in the most obvious places, like right under our nose.

Zen Stories

1

Eka's Heroic Practice

The spiritual successor of Padmasambhava, whose name was . . . Eka, I guess; I don't know how to pronounce Chinese. But, Eka, when he first came to Padmasambhava, as the story goes, he knocked on the gate of Padmasambhava's hut, and Padmasambhava came out and looked at him, up and down, and said, "Phuh! What do you want?"

Eka said, "I want to be a Buddha. I want the teaching. I want to give my life in service to all sentient creatures."

Not Padmasambhava . . . I'm sorry . . . Bodhidharma! I always mix these guys up. Padmasambhava was in Tibet, Bodhidharma was in China. Okay, we're talking about China. Okay?

So, Bodhidharma looks at Eka and goes, "Huh! You know, what you want is very realistic, but you're just some little pup. You're just some little worm! You want to realize that stuff? That's for warriors. That's for heroes. Forget it!" And he slams the door.

Eka understood that if a master as great as Bodhidharma was going to accept him as a disciple there would be some testing involved. He was well aware of that. So he just stood in front of Bodhidharma's hut.

That night there was a snowstorm, and the snow was right up to his waist—to Eka's waist. But he just stood there without moving. And in the morning, Bodhidharma opens the door and sees him out there and says, "Well, that's not bad. But that's not going to make it." Slams the door.

As the story goes, Eka pulls out his knife and cuts his left arm off at the elbow and throws his arm at Bodhidharma's door. This time, Bodhidharma opens the door, takes the arm, brings it inside, bakes it and has a wonderful dinner . . . I'm kidding, I'm kidding!

Bodhidharma opens the door and says, "Clap your hands!". . . No! . . .

He opens the door and he looks at Eka, and he says, "I guess you want it badly enough. Okay, come on in." And he teaches him.

So, there is a time and a place for heroic practice.

COMMENTARY

WHEN I FIRST MET LEE LOZOWICK, I was very passionate about the path, inspired and impatient to get on with the great sadhana that I thought I would be undertaking. For me, Lee as my teacher was the embodiment of everything that I had been seeking for, the one man who could represent my deepest wish to be awakened, and lead me on the path toward that. Nothing else even came close to what I felt for him and the path before me. In short, I felt willing to do anything to engage it, to serve him and to apprentice to his mastery. I was in Eka's position, standing before my teacher's hut, asking for the teaching. "I will do *anything*," I told myself. And I believed it.

So, I wrote a fervent letter to Lee, expressing my feeling and desire to serve him in any way I could. Whatever he recommended, I would do. Some days later, at a large community dinner, he called over to me: "Well, we have three needs here on this ashram—an accountant, a dentist and a photographer." That was it. The rest he left up to me.

I was stunned. I stared at him with my mouth open, nodding to make sure he knew I had heard him, and said nothing. I didn't know *what* to say, because a shocking realization was dawning on me. He had called my bluff, only I hadn't known that I was bluffing. I thought I was sincere to the core. Supposedly, I had been standing there in the snow, ready to cut my metaphorical arm off and throw it at his door. But, as I sat at dinner that night, trying to digest his offer along with my salad, I realized that the thought of being a dentist revolted me, the thought of being an accountant had a shriveling effect on my now quickly waning passion, and the thought of being a photographer was boring and mediocre at best, although the lesser of three evils.

Unable to come to grips with my dilemma—the terrible Yes-No I fell into with his words—I did nothing. I didn't take up any of the three tasks, nor did I verbally reject them, although internally I had definitely renounced them all.

I didn't even have to cut off any body part to put my money where my mouth was. I only had to take up a profession that every bone of my socially-conditioned body dreaded, yet I couldn't do it. If I had been Eka, I would not have received the teaching. But my teacher knew I wasn't Eka . . . not even close. He knew me better than I knew myself, and knew that I didn't yet have the actual ability to stand behind my passionate declarations to him.

Over the years since then I have watched other students approach Lee with the same passionate offer that I had made, and then stumble when a literal opportunity to follow through with it was given. This seems to be the way of things around teachers or gurus. I have also learned that there are very few, if any, Ekas around—men or women willing to sacrifice so much so quickly for the sake of the teaching. Such a level of sacrifice is more likely reached after years of sadhana and maturing in the company of the teacher. Over time, the student begins to learn about himself, begins to know himself in ways and to depths that he or she never imagined. A more realistic relationship to one's aims, wishes and abilities also develops. Sometimes this involves a good deal of sobering, as one's limitations become uncomfortably clear. But only from a more mature place can one have the strength to recognize such limitations and be able to admit to them, as opposed to blindly, albeit with heartfelt sincerity, committing to what one cannot do.

When one comes to a teacher as a student, an apprentice or a devotee, there is always a testing process, only it may look very different in different schools or traditions. For Eka, the test was immediate and harsh. For Milarepa, the tasks of building and disassembling nine houses at the request of his master, Marpa, was a testing process. Such tests are essential steps in beginning the path; essential for many reasons. First, the teacher must weed out the curiosity seekers from those sincerely willing to work and practice. There are plenty of thrill-seekers and spiritual tourists who would be happy to get in on the latest fad with another "high," or a new skill or identity to put on their sleeve. The teacher usually has no patience with this category of newcomer, and will quickly employ means to distract, disappoint or repel them. In ancient times the great walls surrounding monasteries and temples were, in part, for this function of keeping out the idle and curious. In contemporary times, there are other means. Perhaps the seeker pays a visit to a spiritual community and witnesses first hand the challenge of living in a rigorous and maybe even insular situation. If that isn't enough to turn the person off, then the teacher may deliberately present himself or herself as boring, impatient, unintelligent, rude or unappealing, in exactly the manner needed to offend those easily offended or to drive away those who can be driven away. But this is only the first level of a sort of test or screening process.

On many paths, what follows the first meeting with the teacher, whether it is provocative or gentle and ordinary, are the conditions of sadhana required to engage the process that the teacher sets out. These conditions serve as a kind of testing as well. They may include certain periods of meditation, a special diet, the study of specific material, and the adherence to recommendations that might alter one's personal and social life quite dramatically. For some, any sort of rules or conditions of practice will dissuade them from the path. For others, knowing that such conditions exist will encourage and inspire them to delve further.

Whatever methods of testing a teacher may employ, it is not likely in this day and age that one would be asked to stand out in the snow all night, build many stone houses single-handedly, or be expected to cut an arm off. More likely, the demands would be subtle, simple, practical. "Time is the great tester," Lee often says about his own path. "I don't have to do any testing, time takes care of it all. Whoever is left in the end, wins." In other words, a student's passion and dedication to their path must be great enough to enable them to persist in their sadhana for years, even for decades. Probably, one will not be called upon to fight off snow and cold but rather the boredom and distraction of mind that constantly nags at one to jump the fence into the greener grass on the other side, where the action always seems hotter and the rewards greater.

I had and, let's face it, still have a tremendous desire to do heroic practice, like that done in these ancient stories. (Well, maybe I'd keep my arms intact, but a little snow and cold? No problem! A few stone houses? Sure.) Many people in spiritual life share this same passion. But largely, such grand gestures are completely unnecessary. Most such urges to do that type of heroic practice come from mind; they have no tie to the practitioner's actual ability, or even willingness, to follow through. The image of doing heroic practice is romantic; it feeds ego tremendously. The hero archetype is strong, particularly within men, and there are few opportunities to embody it in the world today. Bringing home the check after a week of work in the office just isn't the same thing! So, many of us want to be heroes, with the accompanying recognition, resumé of accomplishments, and self-satisfaction that would come from this.

Nonetheless, Lee tells us in this story that there is a time and a place for heroic practice. What does he refer to?

A student of the French spiritual teacher Arnaud Desjardins once spoke at length about the seeming "glory positions" in the hierarchy of a master's company, noting that many people envy those with closer access to the master, and those who are called upon to represent the master's work publicly. Nonetheless, this disciple stated, "The greatest student lives in the shadow of the master." The *real* heroism, he implied, was not in limelight, but in the corners of the room where the cleaning, or any other less noticeable task, had to be done. For some reason it seems easier to stand out in the snow or to fast for a month than it is to pay attention to one's spouse, be generous with one's friends, put away the dirty laundry, wash the dishes, be patient with a child when you least feel like it. The ability to work silently, invisibly, for years . . . for a lifetime . . . with no demand or expectation for recognition or reward is a rare thing—truly heroic. It is in the corners . . . in the shadows . . . then, that a practitioner's true colors come through. No matter what oaths and promises one has made to the teacher, the true test will be seen in one's daily and practical reliability and integrity as a human being.

Ego doesn't like this arrangement, however. Consistency and reliability mean a slow defeat for pride and self-importance, and a tarnishing of the long-protected self-image. Furthermore, if and when the opportunity for another type of heroic practice comes along, it will most likely not show up on ego's terms, or according to ego's timing. Such an opportunity would not arise from mind but from instinct—from the instinct of the teacher or the instinct of the student, from a necessity and urgency for such action. Only a student who was already aligned with the master or teacher would have the instinct to jump off the cliff at precisely the right moment. And such alignment is earned by preparation, by practice.

When the ancient practitioners in the great stories committed themselves to their sadhana, my guess is they were not thinking, "Well, this is really heroic. I'm glad I'm finally getting the chance to show what I can do." They were probably "sweating bullets," as the saying goes, much as we would when confronted with a seemingly impossible task that would cost us dearly. Yet, for them, there was no other choice but to persist. Their necessity for the truth, for the dharma, was so great that events catalyzed in their lives to bring about the realization of alignment with that which they sought.

Such necessity was rare then, and is rare now, but it is not extinct. One's greatest hope on the path is to find, or more likely "build," such necessity.

2

The Very Disgusting Princess

There was once a prince riding through the jungle who stopped at some woodcutter's hut. The woodcutter's daughter is the most beautiful woman he's ever seen. And, as the story goes, he was a nice prince—not very realistic though. Most princes would have just raped the woman, killed the father, eaten what was in the kitchen and left. But this prince asked the father if he could have the daughter's hand in marriage. Very polite. So the father, also unrealistically, goes and asks the daughter—instead of going: "Prince!? For my daughter? Oh yeah! No more poverty!"—the father goes in and asks the daughter.

"The prince wants to marry you. Please, please, please say yes."

But the daughter says, "Tell him to come back in three days and I'll give him my answer."

So the prince goes away and thinks, "Great, I'll come back in three days."

Meantime, the woman gets the strongest emetics she can find and she starts taking them, taking them, taking them, and everything that comes out of her body—she throws up and gets diarrhea—everything that comes out of her body she puts in these big clay pots.

The prince comes back in three days. "Can I have your daughter's answer?" he asks.

The father says, "She's in the other room."

So the prince goes into the other room and she looks like hell—her eyes are sunken, her hair is all wild, she's unwashed, she stinks. You can imagine after three days. She looks like the ugliest thing he has ever seen.

"Aahhhg!" the prince gasps. "What happened to you?"

The princess points to the pots and says, "That's what you were in love with. Look in the pots."

The prince understands that this is no ordinary woman. This is a woman who understands some deep spiritual truths, so he bows before her and asks to be her disciple. That's how the story goes.

In reality, the prince would have said, "Jeezus, are you fucking crazy? What kind of idiot are you? I'm the goddamn prince! You could have married me! What are you, fucking nuts?" And he would have walked out.

But in the story, the prince understood that the woman was a great woman of wisdom. So . . . it's actually a story about all women, but it's lost on most men.

COMMENTARY

THE FIRST RESPONSE OF "most men" may be to think, "Well, this story ain't lost on *me*! I can see what it's saying." But, unfortunately, it takes more than a superficial understanding of what Lee is pointing at to avoid inclusion in the category of "most men." The story will not be lost on us only if we are living that understanding in this very moment, in relationship to women and men, to life, to ourselves. Piercing the veil of appearances is a difficult and rare achievement, and the aim of most spiritual paths and traditions. It requires the work of years—perhaps decades and lifetimes of discipline and dedication to the sadhana of the path. That veil may lift temporarily in specific circumstances; one may be the prince of the original story at times—understanding the woman's wisdom and able to appreciate it in the moment. Or it can even lift completely, for anyone, when the timing is right for such an opening or shift of context to occur. But Lee seems to be saying one thing quite clearly: "Most men" miss the lesson. Most men are the "realistic" prince of Lee's adaptation: selfish, blind, violent and seeking immediate gratification, whether in the material world or in the spiritual one.

"Most princes would have just raped the woman, killed the father, eaten what was in the kitchen and left." That means us, literally. That is the stuff of our lives, today, here in the twenty-first century. While we may not be raping women and killing children, and taking what we want, literally, we may be psychically, emotionally or mentally raping, killing, and taking what we want. Covertly, we manipulate and control and take advantage of others, aggressively put ourselves first. Or we may subtly assume a position of superiority and pride in relationship to others. But this is just as real—this defines one's life as exactly as the physical act of rape would. As mature as we think we may be, as many years on a spiritual path as we may have had, the primal mechanics of the human mechanism, male or female, are the same as they have always been. Today the social conventions are strong enough to prevent most of us from acting out the more dramatic or violent fantasies, thoughts, or feelings that course through us every day about women, men, life. But those conventions or mores are not strong enough to change our essential relationship to those elements or their effect on us. As Lee's "more realistic" prince, we are continually blinded, seduced and duped by the appearance of things.

To this prince, the woman in the story was meat—attractive, delightful, sweet-smelling meat. Something to be had, nothing more. That's not what he was *thinking*, and that's not what most men are aware of when they first see a beautiful woman, but most of the time that is the ugly reality of the matter. Even a superficial look at history—ancient or recent—bears out in horrifying detail the subjugation, abuse, and repression of women, and of the feminine element in creation that they represent. Today, nothing is different. To most men, women are game to be hunted, captured, used, no matter how sophisticated such men act, or what philosophy they are spouting. Lee is an advocate of the Feminine, and he means this story to upset the men who are hearing it.

Women are continually, in every way possible—whether they know they are doing it or not—trying to reveal something deeper, something more real, to men. This attempt is as clichéd as the man who comes home from work and plops down in front the television, while his wife pines away in the next room trying desperately to find a way to get his attention, to get him to "be with" her, to appreciate who she really is. Women want to be seen, to be known. They want men to be present with them, to stay still for even a moment, long enough for her to reveal herself. Women may be trained and acculturated to attract men's attention with the appearance of their body, the sound of their voice, the way they move and act and smell, but this is only the external expression of the internal yearning to be truly seen, for the very veil that they are presenting to be rent aside and for the essence of Woman to be discovered, invoked, and adored. In this story, the woodcutter's daughter does this effectively by making her appearance so ugly and repulsive that the prince has no choice but to see something else, or not see anything at all.

Men are restless creatures. Most of us are easily distracted, uncomfortable with intimacy and feeling, mechanically seeking to avoid such encounters with reality, while at the same time we harbor a vague sense that we are missing something. That vague sense is also tied to a deeper yearning to know reality, to enter into relationship with that force. Unfortunately, that yearning rarely soaks through beyond the surface. If a man were willing to truly see women as they are—past the social display, the coy game playing, seduction and flirtation; past the makeup and breast size and hairstyle—he would have to deal with a tremendous amount of discomfort. Men are not accustomed to seeing what is real, nor to understanding or accepting it. Rather, their usual response is, to quote the story, "Are you fucking crazy? What kind of an idiot are you? I'm the goddamn prince. You could have married me!"

To get past that response, that primal, mechanical and socially reinforced habit, takes a tremendous amount of work, self-observation and intention. It does not happen automatically upon joining a spiritual tradition, signing up with a teacher or reading some dharma.

The prince of the original story is the ideal prince, the one who understands the woodcutter's daughter when she says to him that he was just in love with shit, not with her. He recognizes his own limited vision and immediately bows in respect to the greater authority, asking to apprentice to such teaching. But most of us, back here in reality, don't recognize that the woman (or man) that we are with is the same great woman of wisdom. More than likely we do not see past the vats of feces, vomit and bile that make up her body, the wart or pimple on her face, the sagging waistline, the bad morning-breath, or her neurotic or eccentric habits, preferences and tastes that rub us the wrong way.

That is the reality of the situation, of our situation, right here, right now. Until this is different in our lives, in our families, in our workplace, in our day-to-day relationships, then the story is still lost on us. Until this is different, we need the foolish ramblings of one courageous enough to put it in our faces, relentlessly, and to keep it there.

3

Milarepa's Last Attachment

There's a story in the Tibetan Buddhist tradition of . . . I'm not sure if it's Milarepa or Marpa. I mix them up because they're all so extraordinary in their own right. So the Kagyu lineage of Tibetan Buddhism began in about the ninth century with a great master named Tilopa. And Tilopa had a student named Naropa, and Naropa had a student named Marpa, and Marpa had a student named Milarepa, and the tradition came from that. And in the biographies of these great masters there are extraordinary stories of the intensity of their practice when they were striving for realization.

And in one case, I'm not sure if it was Marpa or Milarepa, I think it was Milarepa, Marpa initiated Milarepa and sent him off to meditate and to ripen the realization of the initiation and so on. And Milarepa went off for many years and found a solitary cave and meditated. In fact, the cave was so solitary that there was nothing there to eat but thistles.

I know there are thistles in France because I stepped on one in the yard the other day at our place, because I think somehow it's sort of sinful to wear shoes on sacred ground. I don't wear shoes anywhere on the ashram unless there's broken glass or unless I really have to. This is much too rigid a definition for most of my students, but I'm a kind of zealot in some ways, so I do it. Most of my student's feet are too tender to even walk without shoes in the house on rugs, but . . . such is life. They all have these little slippers, you know. But shoes are shoes. Who are they kidding? Well, obviously, they're kidding themselves. But anyway.

Because Milarepa had nothing to eat but thistles, as his biography goes, eventually his skin turned green. That's a very real phenomenon. One of my students, who's very neurotic about his health, used to take vast amounts of vitamin A, as much as he could eat. And he used to eat carrots. I mean just every day—carrots, carrots, carrots! And he actually turned orange.

One day he looked in the mirror because, you know, everybody was joking, kidding him about it. "Hey, you're turning orange."

"No, don't be ridiculous," he said. So he looked in the mirror and there he was, orange.

I keep telling him, "You know, if you're going to live such a neurotic life you might as well be doing it over sugar." Anyway.

So, after many years, Milarepa's initiation matured and he went back to Marpa to seek Marpa's agreement that he had practiced to the extent of the possibility of the practice. And Marpa acknowledged his enlightenment, and said "Now you have to test this enlightenment in life." So he hooked him up with a consort, a woman. Lucky him, because, you know, it was Tibet in the ninth century, so it could have been a yak, or a mountain goat.

Marpa said to Milarepa, "Go and practice tantric practice and come back when that's matured."

In the old days they were tough, you know. And tantric practice was about the union of the masculine and the feminine, but it was completely impersonal. There was no sentiment, no romance . . . nothing like that. Totally impersonal! So Milarepa and his consort went back to his cave. I guess he figured, if he was going to be green, she would be, too. And they practiced tantric sexual union.

This went on for some period of time, and Milarepa's realization was almost mature, but not quite. So he started to fall in love with the woman, in the ordinary way, feeling sort of possessive, like, "This is my woman, my consort, and we love one another." I mean, in those days of course they weren't stupid enough to have such a concept as "soulmates"—which is one of the most absurd inventions of contemporary man known to mankind—or he would have begun to think that this was "his soulmate," the woman that had been created from the same seed of creation in the beginning of time with him; the woman who he has been with in every lifetime and would be with in every lifetime in eternity . . . Dream on. But anyway.

So, let me clean the dripping sarcasm from my voice and go on with the story. Milarepa began to fall in love with the woman, which was undermining the purity of his practice. So Marpa, of course, being . . . omniscient, knew what was going on. Actually, "clairvoyant" is the word I was looking for.

Marpa sent a message to Milarepa: "I have a very important teaching I want to convey to you, so come with your consort."

Oh, Milarepa was very excited. He says to his consort, "Oh! We're going to get another gem, another part of the treasure. Oh, my master is so great, he's so wondrous! He's so . . ." and so off they go.

When they get to Marpa's house, his dwelling, Marpa takes the woman. He takes her in the house and locks the door. Milarepa, he goes crazy. "Oh, my teacher, that son-of-a-bitch! He's in there with my woman! I know what he's doing! The bastard!" He's banging on the door, yelling out to the woman, you know, "Darling! Darling! It's me!" And then, after a while, he realizes that that's it. This is the teaching.

Milarepa goes back to the cave and he starts meditating again. And he perfects the little part of the realization that was impure. Then he goes back to Marpa for acknowledgement, confirmation. And, of course, Marpa, being clairvoyant, knows that he's coming, and opens the door. And as Milarepa comes to his door Marpa runs out and embraces him and says, "Come in, my son, come in! Wonderful to see you!" And gives him back his consort, stuffed, and says, "Now, now you're done. Now you can go."

COMMENTARY

THIS STORY IS SO CLEAR and so typical of Lee's sacred and irreverent blend of teaching that commentary would only dilute it.

One item, however, may enhance its impact. I was puzzled by what Lee meant by "stuffed," as he used it in the last paragraph, so I asked him. He clarified it as a reference to the process of taxidermy. We "stuff" our prize game, mount them on the wall to admire. We keep such trophies around to remind us of our encounters with them. How we triumphed, at last.

A stuffed consort would be a reminding factor *par excellence*, for a monk, eh? Don't pause to question whether this actually happened in the "real" story or whether this is one of Lee's colorful additions. In this story *it happened*. And, harsh as it seems, what other gesture could possibly communicate the reality of nonduality and the necessity of nonattachment as fiercely as this one?

4

Peter's Call

When we offer ourselves to the master in submission, if the master recognizes in us an integrity and a trustworthiness in our offer, then the master makes the gesture. He takes us. He offers us a way to serve him.

You know the story of Jesus and Peter? Peter was a fisherman. Jesus was walking along the shore one day and there's Peter repairing his nets or doing whatever fishermen do. And, you know, Jesus walked up to Peter, and Jesus was obviously totally full of radiance, and Peter's never seen anything like this, even though, of course, there was the historical paradigm of the Jews, which was, "The messiah will come." There wasn't any Christianity in those days. You were either pagan or Jewish, that was it!

So, Jesus walks up and he stands there. Peter looks up and he thinks to himself, "Wow, could this be the messiah?"

Jesus nods. "You got it, Peter."

And Peter goes, "Wow! Cool!" So he says, "Will you come in? Can I offer you some glass of water or something?"

But Jesus answers, "No. Follow me."

So Peter says, "Ahhh, okay. Yeah, I'd love to. Where can I meet you?"

Jesus says, "No, no. Now! Follow me now! This minute; this instant; now!"

Well, Jesus had a soft heart, so he said to Peter, "You can say goodbye to your mother, and then come right out!" Because, you know how Jewish mothers are. Peter would have gotten nailed if he didn't say goodbye to his mother.

So Peter ran in the house, and he called, "Mom!"

His mother came out and said, "Are you hungry? You're too thin. Eat, boubola, eat."

Peter says, "No, Mom. I'm leaving . . . on a fast train . . ." No, actually he just said, "I'm leaving!"

His mother goes, "What?"

"To follow the messiah!"

So his mother says, "What? Bring this clown to me!" I mean, all of this isn't in the Bible, but . . .

Peter brings his mother to the door and there's Jesus. And the minute she sets eyes on him she says, "Okay."

That was it. Peter couldn't have followed Jesus in a million years if Jesus didn't call him to it. People tried following Jesus in those days, and they couldn't do it, except for a few. You know, they say that at the Sermon on the Mount there were thousands of people. How many people followed Jesus? Thirty . . . forty . . . fifty . . . a hundred? We think to ourselves, "Imagine what it must have been like—the Sermon on the Mount, wow!" But there were five thousand people there and most of them didn't give a shit. All they wanted was fish and bread and they were happy, perfectly happy.

"Wow," they said to themselves, "that was a great seminar," and off they went home to fight with their families and their kids. "And the fish wasn't bad either. And, for a minute there I didn't think I was going to get any, but . . ."

Only the master makes the choice about who gets to serve.

COMMENTARY

LEE MAY HAVE TOLD THIS STORY in a small circle of devotees, or just as readily in a large gathering of participants at a spiritual conference in Europe in which he was one of many featured speakers. He may have told it in France or Germany, two staunchly Christian nations. His audience, at times, would have held a few priests or monks, and most of his listeners would have been raised in the Christian tradition, if they were not currently practicing this way.

Lee seems to relish injecting humor and satire into the jugular veins of serious-faced Christians by his own unique renderings of the traditional stories of Jesus. Even those of us who don't think we have much investment in political correctness will often squirm at his outrageous asides and apparently shameless jokes. Amazingly, however, those in the audience whom we might imagine taking the most offense at Lee's approach often come up to him after the talk, thanking him for his work, able to see through and beyond the words to the truth of his message. His "take" on the story of Peter's call to discipleship offers a rare or at least fresh perspective, even to those who may have studied the Christian Gospels in some depth.

With this irreverent account of the conversation between Jesus and Peter, Lee is illuminating a great paradox of the path. Namely, that one must work and practice unrelentingly, with dedication and self-sacrifice; yet, even with this, it is something . . . or someone . . . other than oneself—the master, or God, or the process —that makes the choice about who gets to serve.

As in every story that he tells, Lee is here affirming that practice must become a priority, more important than comfort, or rest, or one's cherished personal and private time. Obstacles must be struggled with, overcome and left behind, and reliability must be developed. As Lee says in the beginning of this story, one must have trustworthiness and integrity in one's offer to serve a master.

On the other hand, "Peter couldn't have followed Jesus in a million years if Jesus hadn't called him to it." So, even trustworthiness and integrity are no guarantee that one will be given the opportunity to follow the master. Lee is pointing to the same paradox that exists around the goal of enlightenment or awakening. That is, no amount of practice, work or effort is any guarantee of results, any guarantee of awakening. In fact, there *are* no guarantees on the path. None whatsoever. No money back, and no thirty-day, or even thirty-year, return policy. Spiritual life . . . practice . . . following a master . . . is one big gamble. If everything is not put on the table, there is certainly no chance of "winning," but even if it is, the chances are still slim. The teacher cannot make promises, no matter how great his love for his students. The teacher can only work in alignment with the greater spiritual force or transmission moving through him or her. Theirs is not a personal choice, nor a predictable one. The teacher cannot pick favorites, although he may certainly prefer and enjoy the company of some over others. The principles of dharma, the principles of karma, the miracles of benediction, and the teacher's resonance to these, determine who gets called to do what, and when. Trying to explain it all may be to undermine or attempt to control the very mystery of the process.

This is not to say that no merit is earned from years of sadhana, or that it is all wasted. *Nothing* is wasted in one's sincere efforts on the path. At least, one might become kinder, wiser, more generous over time. At best, perhaps truly humble, radiant, compassionate. Perhaps the student will come to realize, after all, that the path itself is the goal, dropping all struggles to *get* something or *be* someone.

When new or prospective students investigate a teacher or spiritual school, this checking-out procedure usually takes a common form. The student looks around and says, internally or out loud: "What does this path offer me? What does it claim, what does it produce? What can this teacher offer? What can he or she do for me?" And there is usually a subtle, or not so subtle, feeling-around for guarantees of some kind.

When people approach my teacher as prospective students he is usually quick to counter this "what's-in-it-for-me" mentality with several up-front questions: What can *you* do? What do *you* have to offer this school? What do you have to offer *me*? People are generally taken aback. Who thinks about a commitment to spiritual life in these terms? The usual approach to life—It's all about *me*! How can I get ahead?—is often no different when the consideration becomes the spiritual path. It's still all about *me* (I'm speaking from experience here). Knowing this, Lee wants to impress upon people, from the start, a greater perspective on the matter, a perspective that is aligned with the teaching rather than with ego's agenda.

With these questions—What can *you* offer? How can *you* serve?—the ball is back in the student's court, for the time being. He or she is now charged with developing the trustworthiness and integrity that may earn them greater opportunities to serve. Nonetheless, the opportunities for true service exist only as a possibility. Still, if a student's heart is set—captured by the path and the teacher—no amount of risk, no trials, no demands will discourage him. Everything will be worth it; anything will be worth it. Even the slightest, simplest offer to do something for the teacher or the teaching will be received eagerly.

In India, they say that a true devotee or disciple is like a dog at the table of the master, waiting attentively and anxiously for any scrap, any crumb, that the master might throw them. A true disciple should want to do everything for the teacher—cook for him, do his errands, clean his house, accompany him everywhere, take care of every responsibility—even unreasonably so. That does not mean that they will get that opportunity, or even need to, but such would be the passion and hunger for the teaching.

There's a common maxim of the spiritual life that says, "When the student is ready, the teacher will appear." If one has been looking for a teacher for years, and is still looking, they may question this statement, doubting its validity. But as hard as it may be for ego to admit, it is more likely that one has not found a teacher, or been "called" by a teacher, as was the case with Peter, because one is not yet ready. One may *feel* ready and have felt ready for years, but a true readiness for engaging work with a master is nothing that one can assess for oneself. This can only be assessed by the teacher, and when the timing is right.

The element of timing cannot be understated. As they say in the comedy business, "Timing is everything," and the teacher or master knows this principle intimately. Wrong timing in beginning something can prove disastrous; can destroy a delicate window of opportunity. As a seeker one cannot predict or determine this timing, nor force it to happen prematurely. One can only lean forward into one's disciplines and personal practice with one's intention to become ready. One can work to develop maturity, integrity, reliability—qualities that will be infinitely valuable to a teacher and indeed make one all the more attractive to him or her. Then, when the messiah walks down the shore and says, "Follow me," one will have the clarity to recognize *who* it is that is calling, and the courage and strength to be able to follow . . . at the drop of a net.

5

Parvati's Request

There's a great story in the Indian scriptures. One day Shiva was meditating, absorbed in himself. Parvati, who was his wife, came along and saw him meditating and sort of got this little twinge of question. She punched Shiva in the arm, and said, "Wake up!"

Shiva woke up and looked at Parvati and said, "What? What? We just had sex two million years ago. Can't you wait? Have some patience!"

But she said, "No, no, it's not that." She went on, "Everybody's talking about you as this great devotional God —that you love your devotees, and you're always serving everybody. You know," she said, "you're just absorbed in yourself here. You're not doing anything! Why don't you go down there and serve some people?"

So, Shiva thought he would teach Parvati a lesson. He would have taken her on his lap and spanked her, but then she would have gotten him out of meditation three times a week. Instead, he decided to give her a different kind of object lesson.

Shiva took a big sack of gold, enough gold to have made anyone a king for a lifetime, and he threw it down to earth. Bang! The gold falls right down in the middle of a public thoroughfare, in the middle of the road. And it sits there, waiting for the lucky devotee of Shiva who will come along and find it.

Meanwhile, there's a man walking along, and he's got a crippled leg. He's walking along, dragging his crippled leg, and he's complaining, "Oh, why did God give me this leg? Look at all the healthy people around. Why couldn't I have been healthier? If I was healthy my life would be happy, my life would be different, I'd be rich. Now I can't even get a job, and ohhh . . . ," just complaining and complaining.

And he's cursing Shiva, too: "Shiva, I worship you all my life and what have you done for me? Nothing!" But then he gets this thought. "You know," he says to himself, "things could be worse. I could be blind. Oh, that would be worse." And he thinks, "Let me see how bad that would be," so he closes his eyes and pretends to be blind.

Now, as he walks along the road with his eyes closed, he passes right by the sack of gold. When he passes the gold he opens his eyes again and goes, "Well, yeah, there are some things I should be grateful for. At least I'm not blind."

Then Shiva says to Parvati, "There! Now you understand."

And she says, "Yes, oh Lord," and went back to the kitchen . . .

COMMENTARY

. . . "WHERE SHE BELONGED," presumably. At least that's the inference.

This story is a classic teaching lesson about the blindness of humanity. Yet, Lee adds this insinuation at the end—a comment that is almost guaranteed to grab the audience's attention away from the apparently more serious consideration at hand. Why?

If there's one thing that raises the ire of feminists, and even of most women today, it's being stereotyped in their roles. If there was ever a quagmire of confusion, this one certainly ranks near the top. Lee doesn't hesitate to plunge into this quagmire, however, taking both women and men with him. In fact, he almost seems to enjoy it. He seems to be trying to provoke something in his students or his listeners that's beyond usual definitions of femininity or masculinity, beyond the current popular, but simplistic, stand on gender awareness.

Unfortunately, the important and necessary sexual revolution of the Sixties has turned, in part, into a kind of political correctness concerning gender. Every sentence must include "her" and "his," every social and cultural distinction must be respected. While this is to be expected in the conventional world, those who are looking to observe themselves and their misplaced identifications in the light of a broader perspective will often discover that such investments in politically correct language and non-sexist role assignments are more concessions to mediocrity. A spiritual teacher's job is not to turn his (or her, pardon me) students into strong and powerful men and women. Being strong and powerful as men or women is a prerequisite to spiritual work. The teacher's job is in the creation of practitioners, at least, genuine disciples at best.

When, at a recent seminar, a woman asked Lee, "How can I become a real woman?," his response was to suggest an alternative question: How can I become a real disciple? This, he asserted, was a more far-reaching question, and one that encompassed the first. Yet, such a distinction is seldom made in the spiritual scene, with its glut of men's and women's workshops, drumming circles, goddess retreats, and other well-meaning activities. While a deep bond with and relationship to those of our own gender and a respect for the opposite gender are necessary, they are not a primary focus or aim of spiritual work. To apprentice to a teacher, to enter the path as a student, implies a willingness to transcend our usual identifications with our socially and culturally defined selves.

When any social issue enters the field of the teaching, no matter how important it is and how much merit it may have on its own, it can obscure the purity of the dharma. The study of social change is linear, horizontal. It aims to better things on the horizontal plane. Parvati's request to Shiva seemed compassionate —like any good mother concerned for her children, she wanted Shiva to help out, to *do something*, instead of simply meditating. But the dharma moves in a vertical direction; its aim is to change and transform upward, not forward. Usual definitions of "progress" and "success" do not always apply.

Social causes like feeding the hungry, helping AIDS victims, giving shelter to the homeless, and other such projects have tremendous value in their domain. Such activities can be a perfect venue for practicing the dharma, for putting into action the principles of compassion, kindness, generosity. But if a successful project becomes the primary focus, if the presence or absence of measurable results are used to judge the worthiness of the aim, then a larger and more ultimate perspective may be missed. The heart of the dharma itself can be obscured.

"Social work spirituality" that gets swept up in the gaping needs of the world it is trying to help, slowly but inexorably multiplying *action* without a concomitant attention to *being* or non action, is compromising the integrity of the tradition. The needs of the world *are* endless; the well of suffering, bottomless. The world will always cry out for help. Injustice will always knock at our doors. What is called for is not ignoring it, but placing such suffering within the greater context—the one that Shiva demonstrated in the story. One's life of prayer, service, celebration, devotion, praise of and surrender to God must not be swallowed by the context of the world's needs.

The purity of the dharma must be preserved at all costs so that the transmission is still available, whether via a living teacher, artifacts, or texts, for ages to come. If the texts are all revised to state "her" as well as "his," nothing of real importance may be served. As a student of the path, one must get bigger than such distinctions, rise above having to be identified with "equal representation," and such ideas. The transmission of a tradition—from Israel, Syria, Tibet, India, Japan, wherever—may still evidence cultural and time-sensitive prejudices, but the essential heart of the transmission does not. It is not necessary to dissect and weed out every cultural prejudice before assimilating the teaching. That will happen on its own, in the process of a true dedication and commitment to living the teaching.

Cultural and social prejudices do not stop the true teaching from being available, they only stop mind. One can choose to be thwarted on the path by these things or to consider them within the larger context. One can work to resolve the endless social inequalities and injustices around them, but unless one is also working to undo their source inside oneself, one stays a part of the problem, rather than part of the solution.

6

Mirabai's Beloved

You know the story of Queen Mirabai? When she was four years old, a little child crawling around the house, there was this statue of Krishna. It was painted blue and looked really flashy, and she liked it. She started playing with the statue, and her mother (who was a very religious woman and probably had some dope for a husband who just jumped her bones whenever he felt horny), said to Mira, "Ahh, the divine spouse. Little girl, my darling little girl, if he would be your husband for the rest of your life you'd be happy as an Indian pig in shiii . . . the garbage dump."

Mira, being four years old and loving her mom and being very impressionable, said, "Then that's who my husband will be." And she grew up, and the statue she carried around with her never left her sight, and she began to worship it.

And when . . . this is exactly the way the story went, a direct translation . . . , and when she got to marriageable age —she's royalty, she's in a royal family—her family betrothed her to a prince; very wealthy, very arrogant, used to getting his way, as male sons were in those days. Princes got everything.

So they got married. She was maybe twelve, he was sixteen. They went to the conjugal bed—not when she was twelve, but in a couple of years . . . His whole family thought she was weird. All she did was worship this Krishna all day. And you know, they were Hindus, they understood, but to a point. So, when it came to the conjugal bed and he wanted to sleep with her, she wouldn't sleep with him. And he said, "Why not?"

She said, "Well, I did this for family, but Krishna's my spouse." Just like a lot of nuns and monks take Jesus as the bridegroom; betroth themselves to Jesus.

Mirabai was very beautiful and very talented. She would sing and dance. The prince really wanted to make her his wife, so he tried threatening her, and he tried all kinds of things, but none of it would work. So, he had a couple of choices. He couldn't divorce her—for a prince to divorce a woman, he would really lose face. So he tried to figure out how to get out of the marriage; how to get out of it with face! He couldn't kick her out, because a prince is supposed to be hospitable and generous.

The first thing he does is to send her a . . . What do they call those snakes in India? Not a cobra; there's a much more poisonous one . . . a certain kind of asp . . . in a picnic basket. And Mirabai opened the basket and out comes the snake.

She tamed it! In India! Where snakes are considered to be like dragons—the worst evil. It's funny because, you know, snakes are snakes; if you know how to handle them you handle them, and there's no reason they should bite you unless you don't handle them properly. Mira handled the snake and put it outside.

The prince is really disappointed, so he sent her wine, poisoned, with this great dose of poison in it. Mira, who is always ecstatic from worshipping Krishna, is telepathic, is psychic. She knew that the wine was poisoned. But she just took the wine and toasted Krishna and said, "Oh, beloved Lord, it's your wine. So, hell, I mean, you're either going to take me to you or what's the difference?"

She drank the poisoned wine down. Nothing happened. After that, the prince knew that she was a genuine saint, and he began to worship her as a saint.

Finally, she just took to the road, wearing some rags. She went out with her statue, singing and dancing down the highway: "Hi ho, hi ho . . ." and something about "a yellow shit road," if you've ever been in India . . .

COMMENTARY

THE STORIES OF THE GREAT lovers—like Mirabai and her dark lord, Krishna; Rumi and his beloved Shams i Tabriz; Layla and Majnun; Jesus and Mary Magdalene; and many others—are part of Lee Lozowick's repertoire. He talks often of the exquisite pain of longing for God; the exaltation that characterizes the lives of those who have given themselves completely to Love; the magnificent poetry and inspirational writing that have emerged from such relationships. He writes about these lovers, and related themes, in his poetry to his own beloved guru, Yogi Ramsuratkumar.

The story of Mirabai is a great historical myth, passed on for centuries in India and now even making its way into Western culture. Hers is a story of a love that persists beyond all odds. Such tales need to be told, especially in an age in which "love" is used to sell toothpaste and everything else. And yet, with Lee's rendering, Mira's life is somewhat demythologized in pointed and specific ways that add new elements to the story, making it perhaps more useable to contemporary listeners. We may even find ourselves chuckling a bit as this serious tale becomes delightfully humorous at times. After all, Krishna himself was quite the trickster, playing practical jokes on his beloveds, like hiding the clothes of the cowherd girls who bathed in the river.

And so Lee tells us that Mirabai, crawling around the house as a child, takes a liking to a statue of Krishna because "it was painted blue and looked really flashy." She takes it up as a toy. Well, that's somewhat akin to the way most human relationships begin. We look at someone, maybe talk to them, and we get this feeling—not of love, but of desire: "I want him." "I want her." "He's cute." "She's sexy."

If we're honest with ourselves, our fascination with the loved one is often not much different from a child's fascination with a bright toy, at least in the beginning. For many people, once they've played around for a while with their new possession, the novelty of it (i.e., the new relationship) starts to wear off. The once perfect match becomes a bit tedious; they may start to take the other person for granted, ready for something else.

Mirabai's mother, however, planted a different seed in her daughter's consciousness. Whether her instruction to the child was out of her own great devotion or simply because she didn't want her daughter to suffer her fate at the hand of some dopey husband in some conventional relationship doesn't much matter. She tells her daughter, in so many words: If *that* guy you're playing with now, in the form of a little statue, would be your real husband for the rest of your life, *then* you'd be truly happy.

With this directive from her mother, Mirabai simply and clearly made a decision that Krishna was hers, and she was Krishna's. Not because she was in love with him; not because of his glory, his mythological greatness; not because of the transcendent possibility of divine love, but because she was just an impressionable little girl. She innocently believed her mother. How could she know what that would mean in her life? She was four years old!

Mirabai didn't look at her mother and say, "But Mom, what if he isn't 'the one'?" No. She took what fate offered her—she took this statue around with her, so that it never left her sight, and then she began to worship it. At that point something real began to happen in her relationship to Krishna, not before. Beforehand it was innocent interest, delight. Once she had committed to Krishna, she began to relate to him in a different way. This way of relating slowly began to produce a divine alchemy between Mirabai and Krishna.

Unfortunately, as products of a superficial spiritual culture and a Hollywood-romance-inspired age, we commonly have it backwards—we expect that the alchemy should happen first. If there are no sparks, if we don't swoon or feel some definite "karmic" connection to our "soulmate," then we simply can't imagine that we have found the right person. We're looking for the finished product, the ideal man or woman as they mythologically "should be."

In the Sufi tradition, a story of Mullah Nasruddin conveys this humorous but sad predicament that many fall into when looking for their beloved. One day, as Mullah Nasruddin is sitting around with his friends, one of them asks him why he hasn't yet married, to which Nasruddin replies: "Well, I tried to find a wife at one point. I traveled all around to many cities to find the perfect woman. First, I went to Cairo, and there I met a beautiful, radiant woman."

"Well?" his friend asks.

"Alas, she was not the right woman because she was not interested in spiritual work, so I had to look elsewhere. Then I went to Istanbul, and there I found a woman who was deeply committed to the path. She worked selflessly day and night to serve others and worshipped our Lord constantly.

"Well?" his friend inquires again.

"Alas," Mullah says, "she was not the right woman because she was not attractive and slender. So then, finally, I traveled to Baghdad, where I found the perfect woman: she was young and beautiful and very dedicated to spiritual work. So I asked her hand in marriage."

"And so?" Mullah's friend is nearly breathless.

"Alas," Mullah replies, "she told me no, as I was not the perfect man."

Alas, those who mature in wisdom learn, sooner or later, that there is no perfect man or woman. But a good relationship, a good partnership, can arise out of the imperfection that we all live as. Indeed, a man or a woman will only become "perfect" *after* entering into and persisting in a relationship of worship with their beloved. Not an ordinary relationship, but one of worship, one of adoration, where we are deeply devoted to the other. And, actually, it becomes irrelevant whether the other is worshipping or adoring us at the same time. The object of worship need not return such love for it to be holy or sacred. The lover is transformed in the adoration and worship of the lover, whether the love is divine or human—it makes no difference. He or she is made perfect in their absolute and objective love for the other, not in their seeking to receive, or in their receiving of, that love. That is how Mirabai becomes who she is.

Nevertheless, such a love is dangerous. It consumes and alters the ordinary destiny of individuals. Even in Mirabai's time, surrounded by people for whom Krishna was as common as Jesus is to Westerners, she was not received well. Her consuming love so surpassed her concern for ordinary human life, and so threatened those around her, that her own husband tried repeatedly to kill her. If a similar love were to be displayed so openly today, it too might receive the same response. To ego, anything bigger than itself is threatening and, one way or another, ego will seek a way to undermine or sabotage whatever threatens it. Whether from outside or from within ourselves, a force will always arise to confront the purity of intention with which we head out on the path. This is inevitable. Either circumstances will try to poison us and destroy what we are building, or we will try to poison ourselves, from within. The fire of adoration, of interior worship, must be strong enough to create an immediate antidote to whatever poison is poured into the cup.

For Mirabai, by the time her cultural obligations brought her into the household of a human prince, she had become so transformed in her love for Krishna that she was impervious to poisoned wine or snakes. But then, as Lee says, maybe it wasn't such a big deal with the snake. "Snakes are snakes; if you know how to handle them you handle them and there's no reason they should bite you unless you don't handle them properly." There's not much myth or mystery to that! Again, as our great tale is being told, it is at the same time being demythologized: Mirabai took a liking to Krishna because he was blue and flashy; her mother probably had some dope for a husband who just jumped her bones whenever he felt horny; snakes just need to be handled properly; and India is more likely to have a "yellow shit road" than a "yellow brick road." While Lee consistently presents his listeners with the transcendent, it is usually with a twist that doesn't allow us to get too holy about it. He is quite adept at presenting the divine in human clothing.

Where does that leave us? Still with the divine and transcendent possibility of worshiping the beloved in our partner (or in Krishna). But maybe also open to the reality that our beloved might show up looking a little stiff and wooden at first, not quite so perfect—maybe not even flashy and blue. More than likely, we might appear a bit wooden ourselves. Unconsciously, we probably offer our own beloved the poisoned wine and the snakes for years. Only with time and attention do we learn to see the beloved, our partner, for who they are and to bow down at their feet.

Lee seems to suggest that innocence and trust are the best prerequisites for love, human or divine. In the end, if we, like Mirabai, lose the palace, the fine food and wealth, and end up skipping down the road in rags ("Hi ho, hi ho . . ."), we might not have lost that much at all.

7

Lazarus Is Back

You're probably all familiar with the story of Jesus and Lazarus. Lazarus was dead and he was wrapped in the cloth that they wrapped corpses in, in those days, and he was essentially buried.

Jesus came around, really anticipating their meeting, because he really liked Lazarus a lot. "Where's Lazarus, my buddy, my pal? Where is he? Come on Lazarus! Come on out here!"

Then Jesus looked around and he noticed that everybody was in mourning. He didn't notice at first. He said, "What's up?"

And everybody was crying, "Oh, Lazarus has died!"

Jesus went, "What? Why didn't you tell me? For Christ's sake!" That's how he got his last name.

Boy, I really appreciate you laughing at my Christian jokes, because even though I really honor and respect Jesus, also, it's helpful to laugh about these things.

So, Jesus went to the tomb and he said to everybody, "Wait here."

He went into the tomb and they all thought he was just gonna grieve for his friend. A little while later, out he walks with Lazarus. And as the recorded history goes, the wrap was falling off Lazarus's body and he smelled like a person who'd been dead for three days.

Maybe some people, maybe even some Christians, think, "Well, that didn't really happen."

A story like that is sort of like deifying Jesus, and that's part of the myth, and it's important, very important, for every great person—not just spiritual teachers, but great artists, and great musicians. It's important for every great person to have a myth surrounding their life. Really.

Henry Miller, or somebody equally credible, said, "Never let the facts interfere with the truth."

COMMENTARY

WE LIVE IN THE INFORMATION age, where technology is God. With modern science as the agent of God in all matters, facts have become our idols. We feel security in numbers, in knowledge, in scientific studies, in facts, and in anything written. Our relationship to information is akin to a child blowing a monstrous, towering bubble, which soon threatens to carry him away. It's not that facts are not valuable; they are in the proper context. But facts are the creation of mind. Science, as the result of the body-mind's perception of the phenomenal world, is simply one level of reality. Other levels of reality exist outside of that perception and will never be appreciated by it; never fit into its neat little scheme.

Creation stories will never correspond to modern science's records of how the earth has grown and changed over millennia; and miracles will never jibe with modern medicine's views of how healing takes place. In the world we live in, the facts always seem to get in the way of the truth.

And what is the truth? Is it literally true that Jesus brought Lazarus back to life after he had lain dead for three days? Some would answer absolutely Yes, others would point to the fact that such a feat is impossible, has never been proven, is unlawful to nature. The point is, it doesn't matter. What matters is the truth, not the fact of whether Jesus did this thing or that thing. The truth is that *everybody* is dead, as dead as Lazarus might have been, until they are aroused from that walking death by the call, the grace, the teaching, of one who is genuinely alive. That call, and our receptivity to it, is what matters! That's the message that Lee is reminding his listeners about.

The truth of who Jesus is—as a prophet, healer, visionary, teacher, and embodiment of the divine—is eminently more important than the truth of what he did or didn't do. The life of such a person is invaluable to us today, thousands of years later. His life is a representation of principle—of the principles of compassion, forgiveness, love, integrity, humility, generosity. These principles are the truth. And this truth is a kind of food without which humanity would dry up and starve to death—a kind of emotional-spiritual death.

In the modern world we are starving for the inspiration, the dedication and the uncompromising intention that our mythical heroes, our saints and sages, and many other great figures throughout history have exemplified. That is why their lives are of such priceless value to us. Not for what they did, but for who they were; for the visions that they held and lived by. When such great ones stand out, apart from the status quo that characterizes their times, they are usually quite controversial. Their challenge to the average human manner of living, thinking and being is a threat to all the forces within us that are not willing to take such steps, make such changes, risk so much. Whether they are world leaders, mystics, poets, musicians, writers, political figures or field laborers, such as Cesar Chavez, it does not matter. The example of their lives is like gold to the rest of humanity.

But let's say that one of these great people has had an affair, experimented with drugs, slept around, or done something else that the moral majority (ourselves included) deems unacceptable, or out of integrity. Here we encounter a line—on one side is the fact of what this person did or does, on the other side is the truth of what their life stands for. We have a choice: we can see the facts for what they are, yet continue to be fed by the inspiration and vision of this person, or we can conclude that the evidence of such facts invalidates all their other higher qualities, deeds or commitments. In other words, we can let the facts get in the way of the truth.

Some years ago it came to light that Gandhi, perhaps one of the most inspirational figures of the past century, frequently slept with girls or young women, not in a sexually active way, but physically next to them. Many who heard this were totally scandalized, shocked. Their previous faith in Gandhi as a model to emulate was shattered. Whoever brought this information to light must have thought that they were serving the world at large by having the whole truth be made known of Gandhi's life.

I think they were sadly mistaken. In fact, I think they did a tremendous disservice to the world at large by revealing something that mind, in its weakness, would mechanically grasp onto as meaningful, something that was both irrelevant to the public's image and appreciation of Gandhi and irreversibly damaging to the value that he served in the world.

To the people of Jesus' times, the fact that he fraternized with a tax collector and with a known prostitute and that his disciples picked grain on the Sabbath was enough to discredit him completely among those who held to the letter rather than the spirit of the law. If we search through the lives of every great figure—every saint, every pope, every Buddha, Jesus, Krishna, every historical and current spiritual master—we would undoubtedly find similarly incongruous details, and even "immoral" actions in each of their lives. But we would be wasting our time. Such pursuits in the name of journalistic integrity would be a sham, a sad and terrible blow to the radiance and purity of truth, or of myth. The myth surrounding these individuals, the communication and impression that their lives have on us, whether they are dead or living, is the lifeblood of the soul and spirit of human culture —of what little there is left of it. We must tread carefully so as not to snuff this out, too.

8

Two Monks, a Woman, and a River

There's a story in the Zen tradition: Two monks were walking along and they came to a river crossing. There was a beautiful young woman there, and she was very timid and afraid to cross the river.

One of the monks said to the woman, "Get up on my shoulders and we'll walk through the river, and you'll be fine." And she did, and they walked across the river, and he put her down on the other side, and the monks continued.

The second monk was getting more and more disturbed and, finally, he said to the first monk, "I gotta say this. How could you take that woman on your shoulders? We're monks. You're breaking your vows. This is a terrible thing. You shouldn't have done that."

The first monk said, "That may be so, but I put her down back at the riverbank and you are still carrying her."

So, it's a teaching about mind, and the control of mind and the direction of mind.

That actually happened to me once. I came to a river and there was a beautiful young woman who was afraid to cross, and I remembered the Zen story. I said to her, "Why don't you get up on my shoulders, except facing the opposite direction I'm facing."

Instead of doing it she slapped my face.

I didn't understand it

COMMENTARY

NOW LEE REALLY *HAS* GONE too far—painting his listeners a mental picture of his face in a woman's crotch! Has he no scruples?

Perhaps the better question would be, will we ever hear this old Zen tale again without visualizing Lee's irreverent aside? And beyond that, who among us—earnest practitioners that we claim to be—is willing to admit, as candidly as Lee does, what *really* goes on in the mind while we're looking so holy and appropriate?

Let's face it, everything about our practice of the spiritual path is tainted with our desire to look good so as to be approved by some authority (some "god"?) of our own making. We guard our words carefully; we monitor our expressions; we show up at just the right times; we look shocked when others fail to meet certain standards; the list goes on and on. When are we, as Lee seems to be inviting us by his own example, going to get off our spiritual high horse and start telling the raw truth of where our mind is generally found? "I am simply a master of the obvious, while you are all masters of your neurosis," Lee once told his students.

It's invaluable to be able to laugh at the workings of the mind. It's nothing more than mind that fantasizes about the scenario Lee described with himself. Mind doesn't naturally come to rest on the principles of the dharma, on the nature of compassion or truth . . . yet. It more likely comes to rest on what's for dinner, what's on TV, what we need to do tomorrow, or how it would be to sleep with so and so, or to carry them on one's shoulders facing the opposite direction.

Nothing will make a difference in the power that mind has over us except practice—meaning self-observation, and that without judgment. Nothing else will give us the ability to act differently. We can only observe, with gentleness and hopefully with good humor, the depth to which we are mired in the mud of our own projections, expectations, hopes. We can only note the seemingly unbridgeable gap between where we are and where we would like to be, and then surrender that.

As difficult as this type of moment-to-moment practice may seem, there is no other choice but to persist; to do as much as we can in every moment; to apply as much discipline as we can muster, and then simply to tell the truth about how often we violate our vows and commitments. At that point, we recommit.

There is no replacement for persistence, tenacity and laughter. Often it is simply laughter and humor that both unhinges the rigidity of mind and allows us to move forward past projections and identifications. It's akin to a gust of cool air blowing away the cramped-up stuffiness of habitual mind, which seems to be what Lee is demonstrating in his personal addition to the traditional story.

This story is about all of us. Can we laugh at ourselves? Can we see the absurdity of identifying with whatever woman, or anything else, we are currently carrying across the river?

9

Getting the Secret Mantra

In India there was a great master who was renowned for giving a secret mantra, and there was a young boy who wanted initiation. But the boy was in an untouchable caste and the master was in a Brahmin caste. So the young boy approached the master, but the master wouldn't take him as a student.

The young boy observed the master for some period of time and he noticed that very early in the morning, just as the sun was rising, the master would walk to the bathing ghats to take a bath. So the boy went and he lay down on the steps that led to the bathing ghat.

When the master walked down the steps he didn't notice the boy, because the sun hadn't risen yet, and so he stepped on him. And when he stepped on him, in the master's shock he said the mantra, out loud, because the master was saying the mantra all the time.

When the master realized what had happened he got somewhat annoyed. He said to the boy, "You tricked me." He said, "You've tricked me and it's not right. It's not a formal initiation."

But the boy, who was a wiseguy, said, "Well, you said the mantra with all devotion and all purity, and therefore I received it in the same way, and . . . Too late! I've got it! So lick me," he said. No, he didn't!

When a master has prejudices, there are ways of getting the teaching anyway. You just have to be very tricky, that's all.

COMMENTARY

HOW CAN A MASTER have prejudices? Surely, we might assume, he could not be a true master if he still has prejudices.

Well, maybe not. The common image of an awakened master is one of absolute purity, holiness, gentleness. Leave the mess of human neurosis and prejudice to the students! But if we look more closely at the historical accounts of many teachers, as well as the present day selection, a different picture comes to light. Many teachers or masters demonstrate a range of human eccentricities. Lee has, on many occasions, professed his own human tendencies saying, in no uncertain terms, "I am sexist, misogynist, arrogant, cranky, prejudiced against old and ugly people, and I play favorites shamelessly."

Other spiritual teachers, whether as vocal about their eccentricities or not, nevertheless have them, either overtly or secretly. Scandals about a teacher abusing money or power or sex, in some way, appear in the media fairly regularly.

If we are familiar with the methods and principles of crazy wisdom, a teaching style that utilizes such contradictions to shock and impress students with lessons they might otherwise never get, we might too easily justify all such behavior under that umbrella. "Oh, well, he's just saying that to shock us, for our sake, to make a point." All expressions of prejudice, bias, or mishandling of affairs can thus neatly be tucked away, leaving said teacher on his pedestal. But such a facile labeling would not be doing service to either a teacher or to potential students. It may well be that some of this behavior *does* fall under the category of crazy wisdom, but there is a greater lesson to be gained here—namely, that perfection does not exist in the human realm.

Any teacher, no matter how exalted, is still human, still possessing of tendencies that he or she was raised with. But there is a very important distinction to be considered. If they are a true teacher, no matter how eccentric they appear, these tendencies and prejudices do not interfere with their transmission of the dharma. They may flavor and color the teacher's personality, but the objective ability to transmit the dharma is not so easily affected. And that is the essential function of a teacher—to be an agent of transmission, not some shining example of valiance and nobility.

The individual's typically human manifestations can blind us to seeing their value as a teacher. While some teachers may take advantage of that situation to weed out curiosity seekers, for many it is simply part of the package they present, without apology. Seeing this for what it is, and seeing whether it continues to disturb us or not, is of great value. Perhaps we can begin to accept our own humanness and weakness with a little more compassion, understanding and perspective.

Working against human neuroses need only go on up to a point. Once psychology has enough sanity and flexibility so that it does not interfere with the ability to practice and do sadhana on the path, then it needs no further attention. In fact, further work to try to perfect psychology is a waste of time. However, this can mean that there will still be a host of neurotic or human tendencies remaining, and these can create some discomfort for us, whether they show up in ourselves or in teachers.

If one's desire for the teaching is strong enough, such manifestations will not be critical deterrents. They will merely become temporary obstacles to navigate around; well worth avoiding for the pure dharma that is available beyond them. A teacher's integrity to the outer world is secondary (within limits, of course; we are not talking about murder here, but more the violation of expectations, biases, and social conventions). What is primary is their integrity to the dharma, to the sadhana of their students, and to the transmission of the teaching. If a teacher's integrity to the transmission of the teaching is compromised, then caution is well advised.

Maturity and clarity of vision are required to make such distinctions, however. For the young untouchable boy in this story, there is no question—the master has got the goods, despite his prejudice, and the boy is willing to try some non-conventional methods to get it. As irritated as the master is, his integrity to the dharma is pure, so he can do nothing about what has happened. Even being tricked has a certain lawfulness to it.

The teaching hides behind many obstacles, and creative means of getting past them, not the least of which is trickery, are sometimes called for. That is how to employ one's humanness as a student to navigate around the humanness of the teacher.

10

Nonsen's Cat

There was this Zen monastery, many years ago in Japan, and the roshi's name was Nonsen. This is a true story.

In the monastery was a cat, and the cat lived in one of the dormitories. But there was only one cat, and there were two dormitories, and all of the monks in both dormitories liked the cat a lot.

One day, Nonsen was strolling around the grounds of the monastery and he came upon two monks arguing vigorously. Each of the monks had hold of one half of the cat.

One monk was saying, "This cat has always lived in our dormitory. It's our cat!"

The other monk was saying, "But that's just the point. The cat has lived in your dormitory all this time, now it's time for the cat to live in our dormitory!" And they were arguing back and forth.

When Nonsen walked up, the monks, with good reason, decided that they would let the master solve the problem. So each of the monks presented his arguments very reasonably and rationally to Nonsen, and asked him for his decision.

Nonsen pulled out his sword, cut the cat in half, and walked away. And both of the monks were left to solve that koan.

We don't know whether they have or not, but the koan itself has lasted to this time. It's a very famous koan and it's called "Nonsen's cat."

What it all means, heaven only knows. But there you have it.

I can't make heads . . . nor tails . . . of it.

COMMENTARY

THERE IS SOMETHING REFRESHING in not trying to interpret an action, in not trying to understand or explain something, even though the mind thirsts for it. Some actions are meant to have a visceral impact, cause a shock and short-circuit the mind's grip on the situation all together. Zen masters, in particular, are famous for such actions, and it seems that Lee's own response to the story, clever as it is, avoids taking anything away from the lesson that Nonsen makes.

So saying, I won't belabor the obvious, except to note that Nonsen could have flipped a coin to decide the matter—something we *could* make heads, or tales, of. Instead, the monks got heads or tails, neither of which they wanted, which goes to show that there's more than one way to skin a cat.

And when it comes to the dharma, the best explanation of the teaching might not be the one we're thinking of. More than likely, in fact, if we're "thinking."

11

Gasping for Life

There's a very commonly repeated story—I've heard it both in the Hindu tradition and in the Zen tradition, so I don't know where it started first—where the student comes to the teacher, and says, "I want to know God. I'll do anything."

The teacher says, "Oh, I don't think you have what it takes. It's much too difficult a path. Really, I think you should do something else."

And the student says, "No, no, no! I want to realize God. I've been trying to find Him for years. I've suffered so much. I want to know God!" Very definitive.

At last the teacher says to the student, "Well, all right, come, come, come, let's see where this will go," and takes the student down (the way the Hindus tell it) into the Ganges, the holy river, for a bath as an initiation into studenthood.

The teacher is bathing the student and all of a sudden he pushes the student's head underwater and just holds it there. And the student, at first, thinks "Oh, I'm being baptized," or however the Hindus relate to it.

But all of a sudden the student starts to run out of air and starts to struggle and starts to fight. The teacher still holds the student under the water, and just at the last minute, when the student is absolutely in panic, the teacher lets the student up. The student comes up and gasps for air.

He looks at the teacher like, "You almost killed me! Are you crazy? You creep!"

And then the teacher turns to the student and says, "When you want God as bad as you wanted that breath of air, then come back to me."

With no insult to the sincerity and power of my students, I occasionally think that one of the reasons that I was born as a teacher in America in the twentieth century, and ended up doing the work that I'm doing now, is that when I was that teacher I forgot to let the student's head up above water and he drowned.

I'm being punished.

COMMENTARY

MOST PEOPLE WOULD NOT regard being a spiritual teacher in the twentieth or twenty-first century in America as punishment. Many on the path might even fantasize that such a position is enviable, the ideal place to be, the highest privilege. Just look at the power these teachers seem to have over others; the attention, adulation, devotion given them; the catering to their every whim; the resources, money and gifts lavished upon them. At least this is the way things appear from the outside.

Anyone who has spent some time with a teacher might begin to get a different picture. This is not to say that there aren't plenty of false or not quite integral teachers who are taking advantage of their situations. There always have been, are, and always will be. That is part of the nature of things. But the true teacher lives a life of sacrifice, of surrender to that power that moves through him or her. Such a position is not a personal choice, not a career decision. It is a function that is given to one, perhaps from the lineage in which one works, or from one's own teacher.

To students, the teacher is everything—the greatest, highest, wisest, holiest. But to the teacher, he himself is nothing, no one. And to the universe, to the dharma, he or she is also nothing, no one. Personal life, preferences and decisions all take a back seat to the priority of transmitting the dharma, of working with the students. There is no rest, no vacation, no taking time off from this responsibility. The teacher lives in absolute obedience to the laws of the dharma; to what G. I. Gurdjieff called "objective conscience."

Lee has said that he would not wish this fate upon his worst enemy, but many students and observers still lust after the position. Asked if he was in bliss all the time, Lee replied that he wasn't. He went on to describe the suffering a father or mother feels when their child is sick with measles, or something that is causing the child great pain. He pointed out how, as a parent, one feels both the suffering of the child and the pain at not being able to do anything for them. His experience, he noted, is to feel about ten times that in relationship to his students' suffering and the suffering of the world.

The true teacher or guru chooses to forgo complete absorption into the bliss realms in order to stay in this world, in a body, for the sake of his or her students and their wish to know the true dharma. Thus, he or she takes on the suffering and karma of the students as his work, as part of his function. This is the sacrifice of the guru.

Nothing has changed in respect to this function from the way it was thousands of years ago. That is, nothing has essentially changed. Externally, much has changed. America is conventionally held forth as a great and shining example of the pioneering spirit, of individualism and capitalism, and even of personal freedom and happiness. But this happiness is based upon the superficial and empty attainment of things, like a house, a car, a good-paying job. This freedom is a social or political hype that is bandied about just as long as it does not cross the wrong governmental or political lines, challenge big-enough corporations, or reveal too much of the wrong information. In short, it is a shallow and fragile mockery of an ideal inner freedom, to which it has no relation. Founded upon ideals and principles, America and most of the modern world now cling to the husks of these principles, having long since lost touch with their true meaning. Corporate profit pretty well dominates every sphere of influence—from government, to community development, to music, art, food, education.

With ever more sophisticated technology, the average American's lust for immediate gratification can be met with frightening ease. Discomfort need never be endured, even the slightest. The epitome of this disease is exemplified in what has been termed "the ugly American" by other cultures. Such a label describes the overweight, bumbling, inelegant, obnoxious and greedy tourist. Having no cultural roots of their own, Americans look to nothing more than the commercialized and vapid excuses for Christmas, Easter, or Thanksgiving holidays, the nightly worship of the news or the latest popular television program, the weekend sports pilgrimage, and the daily pain relief offered with caffeine, nicotine, alcohol or valium. Religion serves to sedate any minutely nagging sense of "something missing" by offering a quick salvation through a passionless, once a week, church service; or by reassuring all that giving money will help atone for any sins, thus guaranteeing a blessed afterlife. If one does not like *that* offer, there is another one for sale down the street, or on television, or through the Internet. If Christianity doesn't do it, Buddhism, or Islam, or some New Age spirituality are just as accessible, and make just as many attractive promises. "Spirituality" has become another supermarket commodity, as religion is. Most approaches to this current trend demand little or nothing from the average person in return for the easing of conscience and the insidious stroking of ego.

Into this morass of the Kali Yuga, the age of darkness, as our times are called according to the ancient Hindu calendar, come many teachers from many traditions. And, as if work with ordinary human mechanicality and identifications weren't enough, a teacher today must deal with a climate of self-indulgence and decadence rivaling ancient Rome; with a culture (which can't rightly be called a culture) that kills any signs of essence and innocence in children by the age of three, if not sooner; and with an information system that sucks away any further possibility of self-knowledge by assaulting people with an endless stream of media images, demands to conform, and a worship of materialism.

Most people on the spiritual path come to a teacher with a degree of psychic and psychological wounding that teachers in ancient cultures never had to deal with. Often this psychological ill health must be dealt with before any real work on the path can even begin, and that may require years. Even after considerable work-on-self, and practice, and input from the teacher, such psychological wounding can resurface and, temporarily at least, inhibit further progress on the path. At this point the student must work, usually with help, to heal or repair enough for sadhana to continue. This intervention often becomes the teacher's responsibility, a further burden to his or her already tremendous load.

Even if someone is basically well-balanced, Western psychology has no reference point for apprenticeship, for self-discipline, for obedience or deference to any authority above itself. Even spirituality has succumbed to this pervasive mentality, epitomized by the sentimental perversion of the word "guru" into the moniker G-U-R-U (Gee, you are you). Most seekers are convinced that there is no need for any external spiritual guide or authority, that their "inner voice" is the true guide. Unfortunately, the inner voice is usually the inner voice of mind, not the inner voice of objective clarity. Thus, the teacher must dismantle this false and childish reliance on yet another manifestation of mind in his work to lead the student to a true maturity and wisdom.

If the job were easy to do, and easy to get, there would be thousands, or even millions more spiritual teachers. If it were the aim of the path to become a teacher, there might also be many more. However, this is *not* the aim of the path, but rather a function sometimes given to one coincidental with the realization of the aim of the path.

The aim of the path is to duplicate the *state* of the teacher, not the *function* of the teacher. If the state of the teacher is duplicated, one may begin teaching or simply resume what one was previously doing. But it is the state of the teacher that allows for his function of teaching to be present, not the other way around. One can prematurely assume the function of teacher for oneself, but this will essentially mean nothing and bestow nothing if such a function does not arise out of a lawful and practical relationship to genuine spiritual authority. In relationship to that authority, even the realized teacher is still a student, whether that authority—their own teacher—is still living or not.

12

Moses Gets Out

I'll tell a story somebody told me about Moses and the Jews leaving Egypt. I don't know anything about this, so I can only relate the story as I heard it. Since I heard the story several weeks ago, I've also probably forgotten half the details, so it may be wrong. But, anyway, you'll get the idea.

When Moses and the Jews left Egypt, it was under a very particular circumstance. They didn't leave because they were suffering under the slavery of the Pharaoh, because the Jews and other races had been suffering under the tyranny of the Pharaoh for hundreds of years, and that was not inspiration enough to leave Egypt.

Pharaoh told Moses that he could take the Jews and leave Egypt, and Moses said, "Wow! Wow, that's great. We'll have to talk about this. We'll have to have some meetings and discuss it." But there was no movement going on.

Then, Pharaoh started to think that he'd made a mistake. He started to think, "Maybe I shouldn't let them leave." And the more Pharaoh started to think, "Maybe I shouldn't let them leave," the more Moses thought, "Maybe we should leave."

Finally, Pharaoh said, "No, you can't leave."

And then Moses said, "All right then, we're gonna leave!"

Moses left, and Pharaoh sent his army after them to kill them, or bring them back, or whatever. Then there's all the rest . . . and the sea parted and Moses went through and Pharaoh's army went into the sea and the sea closed up and they all drowned . . . And then there was something about a pillar of fire, a burning bush, commandments and a golden calf and all that stuff.

Later, Jesus came. He was the son of God, and a good-looking son he was, too. God was very proud of him, with all that long hair and beautiful beard and blue eyes. So. "Blue-eyed soul brother" they used to call him in those days.

Now the Black-American Blues musicians use that phrase for any white person who actually has a little bit of soul. It's rare, but every once in a while you find one. They call them "blue-eyed soul brothers."

So anyway.

One thinks of Moses as being a great servant of God and a great recipient of grace and all of this. But, actually, no one thinks of Pharaoh as being a great servant of God. If it wasn't for Pharaoh's behavior, Moses wouldn't have taken the Jews out of Egypt. And then where would history be? Then we'd all be living in pyramids now and writing on papyrus. In fact, most of us are, I think.

COMMENTARY

"I DON'T KNOW ANYTHING," proclaims Lozowick, as he launches into this narrative. Once again we are confronted by a style that seemingly disregards historical accuracy, mixes details, and uses every opportunity to make jokes; in this case, poking fun at Jews and Christians alike. His light-hearted banter about black musicians and blue-eyed soul brothers juxtaposed with the Egyptian desert experience of Moses and the children of Israel lands us in some surrealistic dream sequence. By the time Lee gets to the punch line of his story—if indeed there is one here—we have five or six subplots to the tale, each raising a slew of questions.

Lee's last assertion about the role of Pharaoh in the history of the Jews is intriguing. He echoes sentiments expressed decades ago by Gurdjieff, who said: "Someone had to be Judas. People who do not understand this now ask how Jesus could be with this man for years and still not know him. Was Jesus idiot? . . . Jesus not idiot. There must be Judas." (Rina Hands, *Diary of Madame Egout Pour Sweet*, Aurora, Oregon: Two Rivers Press, 1991, p. 7)

Certainly it is ironic that if it weren't for Pharaoh's behavior Moses might not have taken the Jews out of Egypt. Yet, if Jesus had not been crucified there would have been no glorious resurrection, and his impact on the world may have been far less. If Buddha had not chosen to sit under the bodhi tree until he nearly starved to death, would he ever have awakened?

According to the cosmology of the Fourth Way, the system that Gurdjieff established, there are always three forces at play in the world, and present within every event, every person, in every circumstance: the affirming force, the denying force, and the reconciling force. On the spiritual path, for example, we might say that the affirming force (the "I want" according to Gurdjieff) is embodied in our great passion for sadhana, our inspiration, our determination and clarity. The denying force (the "I do not want") is found in our resistance, our struggle against the very things we long for, our struggle with our desires, our selfishness, our greed, our laziness. The third force (sometimes called the reconciling force) is that which stands between the Yes and the No, keeping a constant state of dynamic tension between them. Whoever or whatever controls this third force commands the difference between mechanical existence and conscious activity. Applying this paradigm to the process of sadhana, we might say that progress often occurs with two steps forward, one step back, little by little, and lots of struggle in between.

Without the resistance of the denying force to push against, there would actually be less motivation to push at all. Things that come easy are just as easily taken for granted, quickly forgotten or uncared for. If Pharaoh had simply left things as he first stated them, allowing Moses to take the Jews out of Egypt, they might have relaxed, become soft, and let years, or even centuries, pass without feeling the necessity to do anything. But it was the denying force—Pharaoh's change of mind—that created the sudden urgency to leave.

The denying force is a necessity, and it is inescapable. In the popular mentality and world consciousness, such a necessary force has been demonized, labeled "evil," or at least considered to be somehow wrong. Don't we all feel this? Don't we turn ourselves inside out and upside down trying to avoid the stuck places? Don't we question what we've done to deserve some setback or some change in the weather? But this denying force, in the myriad forms in which it shows up, is simply part of the physics of the universe. And a better understanding of this dynamic would render it useful instead of toxic.

After leaving Egypt, the Jews endured, and have since endured, endless trials and persecutions. But if one considers the Jewish people as a whole, it might be fair to conclude that their history of suffering has strengthened them, deepened their bond to each other and to their roots, and crafted resilience, intelligence and personal power in them. Common traumas and disasters bring other communities together every day, invoking unimagined generosity, heroism and personal sacrifice. But, without a greater context of work-on-self, such qualities quickly fade with the reestablishment of ordinary life.

Consciously struggling against one's own tendencies toward "sleep" or inattention builds something—an invisible substance within one's being that does not dissipate easily. Spiritual practice builds this substance, as practice is usually a struggle to some degree, an action contrary to the mechanical nature of ordinary life.

A spiritual teacher, as a master of skillful means, will catalyze this denying force in a way that directly serves his or her students. I have witnessed this in my years of observing Lee Lozowick. While encouraging students to abandon unnecessary and self-created struggle—the suffering that arises from personal neurosis and a psychological overlay on life—he seems to be provoking further struggle with more necessary things all the time. My own conflict between my wish to practice and my resistance to practice, between my internal Yes to the teacher and my No to the teacher, continues to happen as Lee is always coming up with some new plan that interferes with my plans, or as he raises the bar on diligent practice once again.

There is tremendous value in being put in such a position—"between a rock and a hard place," as the saying goes. Until I am up against my resistance in all its heat and fierceness, my movement forward is really only a simulation, a walk on a treadmill. Genuine transformation lies on the other side of the fire, and the way there is through the middle of that blaze. Through the suffering of life as a human being, endured consciously on the path, a subtle force is built.

Gurdjieff spoke of this force as that which can eventually build a soul—an essential, subtle body that does not die after the physical body dies. In Gurdjieff's work with students he stated that human beings are not born with such a subtle body, with a soul, in contradiction to popular religion and philosophy which states that everyone has a soul. Gurdjieff taught that a soul must be built, literally forged through the fire of conscious suffering and personal sacrifice. The force that is acquired through struggle is not acquired by any other means, cannot be given by the teacher to the student, cannot be done for them. It is an inescapable law of spiritual work that cannot be circumvented. Teachers and schools of study that offer quick and easy salvation for little time spent, or without any effort required, mislead not only others but themselves.

Lee has reiterated many times that we need not search for suffering. Rather, the conflicts that sadhana and daily life commonly create are enough substance for work, as these generate adequate tension and heat to forge the inner vessel that can hold the substance from which to build a soul. In the company of a living teacher or master, those things that must be struggled with will be obvious and unavoidable. If we are working with a group associated with a teacher, the unconscious manifestations of others will always irritate us, providing an unending source of possibility for working on ourselves, no matter how enlightened they are, or we are. E. J. Gold, a contemporary Fourth Way teacher, has said: "The single greatest technique for work on self is to endure the unpleasant manifestations of others without resentment, expressions of displeasure, or the demand for intelligence, reason, justice or conscience on the part of others. Endure silently and cheerfully, and suffer in the stewpot of tension." (E. J. Gold, *The Lost Works*. Nevada City, Calif.; Gateway Books, 1994, p. 109. Reprinted with permission.)

If this context that Gold refers to is held in the face of the struggles that life and the path will present, then such struggle will not be wasted. The stress of working with others in this way will not sap one's energy and life force, nor reduce one to a bitter, pessimistic and resentful shell of a man or woman.

Without our own pharaohs we would have no reason to mature beyond the reactionary state. Without suffering, there would be no motivation to transcendence. Without prison bars, no desire or movement toward freedom.

The Jews might still be in Egypt.

13

Through Bankei's Keyhole

Bankei was a very, very famous Zen master, maybe twelfth century . . . something like that. He was very sickly as a child, very weak, and he got into Zen practice both as a way to strengthen his body and also as a way to realize the nature of reality. He practiced very hard.

Bankei became a monk as a teenager—at fourteen or fifteen years old—and at forty-four years old he still had realized nothing. Not only that but, as the history books describe, he had a form of . . . what do they call it? Tuberculosis. And he was dying.

He had a little hut. He was in his hut and he knew he was dying. He was kind of embarrassed, and didn't want to trouble people unnecessarily, so he locked himself in his room. One day he went into a particularly strenuous coughing fit in which he literally felt he was dying in that moment. And he hacked up this gigantic black wad and he spit it on the wall. He looked at this black wad dripping down the wall, and he was in that state where he had nothing to lose, and he woke up. Totally and irrevocably, instantly!

Bankei didn't know what it was—he didn't know he was awake. He didn't know what happened. All he knew was—all of a sudden everything had changed. His perception had changed dramatically.

Before this instant he was totally despondent and going: "I've spent twenty-five, thirty years practicing as a monk and nothing has happened. I've wasted my life. I could have been out drinking and dancing and sexing. What has it all been worth?" Basically, he was completely disillusioned.

After this instant he started looking for his mind—his mind that had been plaguing him, but it wasn't there. He was completely at peace. So he thought to himself, "At least I'll die in peace. That's nice. I wasn't looking forward to dying with all these terrible thoughts, all this negativity."

Bankei lies down on his bed, ready to die, and all of a sudden he realizes that he has all this energy; he doesn't know where it's come from, and he doesn't feel like dying anymore. Then another sensation arises—he's really hungry. He hasn't eaten in weeks, except a little milk, a little tea. He's hungry, he's really hungry.

He has this bell, and he rings this bell vigorously for his attendant, who thinks, "This is it. This is his death rattle. He's calling me at last." And the attendant runs in and there's Bankei sitting on the bed looking healthy and radiant, going, "I'm hungry! Bring me rice!"

How did he get in the door, you ask? Because I said that the door was locked. That's the second riddle.

Well, the attendant knew how to pick locks. He looked around the room and there was no wire anyplace—wire to pick the lock. In those days the locks were pretty big, so he took off his pants and stuck his thing in it. He'd been a monk for fifteen years, and he woke up also.

"At last!" he said. "I've found the key!"

Bankei recovered his health completely. In fact, he lived into his eighties, and he went traveling around the country to test his newfound enlightenment to make sure that it was the satori that he'd always heard about and been told about in his Zen practice. Bankei is, at least in the West, renowned as one of the greatest Japanese masters in the history of Zen, alongside of Dogen, and people of that stature.

I don't know about how famous he is in Japan—maybe nobody even heard of Bankei. Maybe some translator got ahold of his stuff and just made him into a famous master. I mean, after all, who do you think put Andrew Cohen's old teacher, Punjaji, on the map? Westerners. Rajneesh? Westerners. Swami Muktananda? Westerners.

COMMENTARY

"AT LAST! I'VE FOUND THE KEY!" . . . as if hacking a black wad of goo onto the wall wasn't a weird enough way to wake up! And, with that, Lee has our attention.

With these ending remarks, Lee takes a broad swipe at the materialism of the current spiritual scene—namely, the tendency of Westerners to "market" their teachers and gurus. This is an opinion that Lee expresses frequently, and without apology. His stance is: To promote the dharma in a large and glossy format for mass distribution, one must either water it down to such a degree that compromises its value, or else risk offending a large percentage of the very people one is trying to attract.

The true teaching is not easily packaged for sale. More likely, the principles of such teaching will fly in the face of ego and the habitual sleeping life that ego is identified with. A watered-down version of truth is not truth. Nor does such an approach do the general public a service, but merely offers another means to delude people into thinking they actually have *something*, when all they hold is the brochure. The dharma prostituted to the lowest common denominator means the death of the dharma. Furthermore, when a spiritual teacher gains the recognition and attention of a movie star, the real work is threatened. Adulation and attention are so seductive—not only for the teacher, but certainly for those in the teacher's company. Vigilance can be lost and small compromises can slip their way into the traditional forms.

Religion may be the opiate of the people, but the spiritual path is not (and can never be) for the masses. When it appears that the masses are taking up the traditional paths (like the widespread fascination with yoga that we see today), then those paths are not far from becoming religions in the worst sense of the term. When the age-old questions of purpose and meaning that humans have always confronted show up as headlines on the covers of popular magazines, one can predict with fair accuracy that their treatment will be superficial, sensational, or completely idiotic. A recent issue of a mega-selling woman's magazine was dedicated to the topic of surrender. Among other things, the lead article featured a checklist of suggestions for "How to Let Go," one of which was, "Lose those extra pounds you've wanted to lose for years."

As Westerners, we have to guard against expecting spiritual teachers to be "slim and attractive," too, in whatever domain currently bespeaks worldly success. We must beware of courting and encouraging such standards. At times, as Lee demonstrates repeatedly in his public persona, it might be necessary to directly discourage and prevent such success so as to preserve the integrity of the teaching.

There has always been a need to separate the curiosity seekers and spiritual tourists from the serious seekers on any path. Many ancient monasteries and temples were surrounded by a high and impenetrable wall. No individual who did not qualify would ever make it past the first gate. It was unlawful. Gaining entrance into the inner courtyards of such places depended on the seriousness, maturity and refinement of one's practice, on one's necessity for the deeper teaching, and on one's ability to use that teaching.

On the exterior of many churches and cathedrals in Europe one can see the sculptures of gargoyles, which served the function of channeling rainwater as well as warding off evil, thus preserving the sanctuary, the precious artifacts, and the people within. Today, few spiritual schools have high walls surrounding them, or stone gargoyles on their fences or walls. However, the need is as great as it has always been for this function to be fulfilled. The teaching needs to be protected from the unconscious mass of tourists, spiritual shoppers and psychic tomb-raiders.

This protective function may be accomplished in numerous ways, from the simple and yet demanding lifestyle that is required of adherents, to the human manifestations of the teacher. When Westerners are caught by the desire to make their teacher or their path more popular, these rough edges and irritants are often smoothed away.

Sadly, one can see the effects of this watering down everywhere—it is now becoming hip, cool, a mark of prestige to call oneself a Buddhist, and in some quarters the label "Sufi" has the same effect. Such religio-cultural diffusion is already influencing language, art, education, and the way people think. But will it ever really change who people are? Ever alter their primal and unconscious relationship to life? I think Lee Lozowick would say not. His appeal is clearly for the necessity of serious work in the crucible of a teacher-student relationship; one that requires a life-altering commitment, not just a casual association.

Human nature will always pervert and distort the true teachings to serve its own ends. Any widely spread teaching will tend to become dogmatic and rigid, or fluffy and meaningless. It is the responsibility of every individual in whose hands the dharma now rests to see this eventuality and do everything possible to preserve the essence, the integrity and the sanctuary of the true teaching.

14

True Prayer?

Isn't there an example in the New Testament in which Jesus converts someone and they're so euphoric that they say, "My Lord, I'll shout your name! I'll pray in the marketplace!"

And Jesus says . . . What he really said was, "Don't be a fucking ass!"

It doesn't say that in the New Testament. In the New Testament it says something like, "True prayer is prayer in private. So you go to your home and you pray in the closet." (He actually said "in the water-closet," but it doesn't say that in the New Testament either.)

I don't mean to disparage Jesus; he was obviously a singularly great master, but the New Testament was not an entirely accurate view of his ministry, as I'm sure most of you know.

COMMENTARY

TO READ OF JESUS SAYING, "Don't be a fucking ass!" is like letting a blast of fresh air into a very stuffy room. That stuffy room is centuries of crystallization around a religious dogma and a stilted image of the life of Jesus.

Jesus was a radical master—wild, fierce in his demands on his disciples, and uncompromising in his teaching. Today, however, he is depicted commonly in only one of his manifestations—as the loving, kind and gentle savior figure. But it's likely that he was more than able to kick some ass when that was needed.

If such portrayals—of Jesus, any spiritual master, or any topic associated with religion—offend and insult, they are rubbing up against a human tendency to take things too seriously. Humor is essential to life. A healthy sign in a teacher or a student of a spiritual path is a good sense of humor, especially concerning him- or herself. If one cannot laugh easily, cannot see the absurdity in one's own foibles, projections and struggles, and cannot appreciate satire about the things he or she most loves and cherishes, that is a dangerous sign. It reveals a personal and egoic identification that cannot be loosened from mind's grip. One can be very serious about the work one is doing without taking oneself seriously at all. An important distinction!

To err is human, but to lighten up a little—
is divine.

15

Ikkyu Awakens

There's a great story, one of my favorites, about a Zen master . . . this could have been Ikkyu, who developed a whole system of Zen called Red Line Zen.

Same thing, you know: Eleven years old; he's dedicated to the path; he wants to realize enlightenment. He goes to the monastery and becomes a monk, and practices and practices hard for twenty years and nothing happens.

Finally he goes to his master and he says, "I've been meditating for twenty years; I've been working and studying my koans, and nothing's happened. So the hell with it, you know?" He said, "I'm thirty"—whatever he was, "thirty-one, thirty-two years old," he said, "my life is almost over," because in those days they died young. He said, "You know, I've got to experience life before I die. I've been in the monastery twenty years, since I've been eleven years old. I've gotta go out and I've gotta get some experience!"

And the master said, "Fine. Okay . . . see if I care." The master said, "Well, all right, then! Fine! Hurt my feelings. Go ahead!"

So Ikkyu's walking down the road, and he's been practicing twenty years and he's totally frustrated because nothing's happened, but he's bright, beautiful. He can't see this in himself, but one thing about twenty years of hard practice is he's pure, he's radiant with his practice.

He passes a whorehouse and the whores look out and here's this beautiful, virginal, radiant, handsome young man walking by. And they're like, "Wow, man! Come on in, fella!"

And Ikkyu said, "I'm just a monk. I've no money, you know. I just left the monastery. I've never been with a woman."

Telling a prostitute that is like waving a red flag in front of a bull, you know. So all the women look at one another and they say, "Let's give this guy a freebie, you know." And to Ikkyu, "Come on in!"

Ikkyu goes in, and the minute he opens the first woman's legs he wakes up. A true story! He figured, "Well, I'm already here. Why waste it." And then when he was done, he walked across the street and he opened up a zendo.

He would sit zazen all day, and then he would go and spend all night at the bordello.

At first he was considered to be some kind of mad heretic or something. People were very disturbed because they thought, "This is not appropriate behavior for a religious man."

But slowly, slowly, people began to sit with him and began to realize that he really had something. And people would ask him, "How could you be a Zen master and also be in the bordello?"

And he'd say, "It's the same."

A lot of people have tried to prove that since. Not as many have been as successful as Ikkyu, of course.

COMMENTARY

THE NUMBER OF WORKSHOPS and seminars today that advertise ecstasy and even enlightenment through tantric sex is growing, and Lee is generally ruthless in his criticism of these aberrations of the dharma. Here, however, he is gentle, at least in his sarcasm, as he concludes, "Not as many have been as successful as Ikkyu, of course."

Why this uncharacteristically mild comment on Lee's part? Perhaps he doesn't want to undermine the wonder and paradox of Ikkyu's ability to live in the zendo by day, the bordello by night.

This archetypal tale illustrates the kind of balance that the Baul stands for—to be fully awake in the world, celebrating his humanness, finding God in, and with, and through the body, while at the same time fully dedicated to his practice of worship. The character of Ikkyu presents exactly the type of paradoxical relationship to life that humans face in our world today. Lee is no stranger to this paradox. He travels for three or four weeks a year in Europe with SHRI, the Blues band formed within his community in 1994, as they play at Blues festivals, in smoky bars, and in street fairs from Norway to southern France. Lee is their lyricist and one of the lead singers. When he puts on his black sunshades, pulls a chair up on stage, draws the microphone up close to his lips and starts to moan a line from an old Blues standard, calling upon the "Angel of Mercy," he is embodying the very ordinary and raw human condition, where ecstasy and suffering live side by side. An hour later he could be seated serenely, dressed in an Indian shawl, and giving dharmic discourse to a group of renunciates. This is the paradox of the guru, whose ability to live in both the world of the ordinary and the mystical, to combine the sacred with the profane, is a demonstration of the teaching itself.

In the guru's world there is no contradiction between contemplation and action, Blues music and Hindu chants, sex and prayer, underworld and upperworld. Genuine tantra is the non-rejection of all things. Not the indulgence, but the non-rejection. Ikkyu lived this teaching. And what better way to demonstrate that but for Ikkyu to balance his time in the zendo with time in the bordello?

Lee also likes this story, I think, because of what it says about striving after results. I know the syndrome well. Like Ikkyu, I want something to show for my efforts. I want to know that the sacrifices I make for practice are getting me somewhere; that I am attaining something.

On one hand, a certain impatience with regard to one's spiritual work is invaluable—it inspires an urgency to work and practice harder. But looking for results can become a real trap, for many reasons. Basically, the results *I want* are big results. I want liberation, complete and unequivocal and right now. I want to surrender to the will of God, in one motion! Or maybe I want to be my teacher's right-hand man, or dream of being sent off on some great mission as a reflection of my advanced accomplishment as a practitioner. The results I might expect and long for are not necessarily going to show up in the ways that I expect. Like Ikkyu, I don't see myself clearly. Nor are my hoped for results necessarily the ones that are most needed.

On some level, karmic or other, merit *is* earned through a life of practice, and things do change, and even transform. Results do show up—but much of this change or transformation is undramatic, untraceable and sometimes invisible. If I look back over the last few years in the company of my teacher, I see that I am less inclined to spend hours in worrying about how I can speed up my progress toward enlightenment, or position myself and my life for maximum spiritual success ("progress" and "success" being precisely antithetical to the nature of the teaching). I am more likely to attend to what is in front of me, taking the opportunities that are given, be they in caring for children, writing a book, or simply managing my livelihood with as much integrity as I can. If "big results" show up at all, they may show up years down the road, as happened for Ikkyu. Twenty years of dedicated practice brought him to the brink of enlightenment as he stepped out of his monastery thinking that he was leaving the path for good. No one and nothing could have predicted such timing, nor the event that catalyzed the awakening for him.

Lee Lozowick teaches that the context of practice is not success or attainment, but resting in the present moment *as it is*, complete with all of one's personal struggles and failures, dreams and inspirations. The context of practice is one of sanity and enlightened vision, clarity and maturity. One practices because there is no other choice. A life of practice is not a means to an end, but is the very aim itself. There are no rewards on the path for good deeds or great commitments—as practice is its own reward.

The influence of the lineage, the teacher and the teaching may be working their way into the subtle levels of one's being for years, or decades even, before anything remarkable shows up on the external level. But, as Lee has reiterated, a life marked by kindness, generosity and compassion is utterly remarkable in itself!

Furthermore, if one is impatient and quick to judge his or her life by some ego-determined set of results, the work begun or already accomplished can be endangered. It is all too easy to run away from a slow-burning, long-term commitment in order to find another more attractive path that promises the quick fix.

16

Zen and the Art of Duckhunting

There was a Zen master who lived in a small town in Japan and he didn't have any particular issues about life. He just kind of went along and took what came and did what he could and so on. The man was a monk and he lived alone and he sat and he did his practices and didn't bother anybody and nobody bothered him.

One day this very attractive young woman, who lived next door to the monk, got pregnant. She was unmarried and the town was very angry. She didn't want her boyfriend to get in trouble, so when people asked who did this, she said, "The monk next door; he snuck in while I was asleep one night."

The whole town went in an angry mob to the door of the monk and they banged on his door. He opened the door and they all started yelling, "You seduced this poor young woman and now she's pregnant!" and on and on.

The monk just looked at them all and said, "Is that so?"

They said, "You're going to have to marry her and be responsible and so on."

And so he did. She lived with the monk for a number of years, and he took good care of her and raised the child, and they had other children together.

After many years, she felt great remorse that she had gotten this poor monk into all this trouble. And she also began feeling like her boyfriend who had run away really deserved to be named. So she called the town together and she said, "In my youth and in my ignorance I was scared and I lied and actually this good man was not the father of my child, but it was so and so." I think his name was Heyoki Misogi. The boyfriend, not the monk. Or was it Iyogi Heyoki. Anyway, it's an irrelevant detail.

Now the town all went to the monk very apologetic and said, "Oh, she finally confessed that it wasn't you, and we're so sorry . . . "

And the monk just looked at them and said, "Is that so?"

This monk was later reincarnated in contemporary times in the city of Munich, and he was out hunting duck in the country. I'm only telling this story because there are several people here tonight that weren't at the seminar and didn't have the benefit of the value of this story. So, I want you to understand that's the only reason I'm telling this story.

This city man was out in the country in the woods and hunting duck. He shot a duck and the duck fell somewhere and the man went to look for it. Well, he comes upon this old farm, and there's this farmer standing there holding the duck.

So the city man says, "Ah, excuse me, that's my duck. I was out hunting and I shot him and that's my duck."

The farmer says, "Well, it fell on my property and I'm the one who's holding it. It's my duck."

They get into a little argument and finally the farmer says, "Well, listen," he says, "I'll tell you the way we settle disputes out here in the country."

The city man says, "All right, I can play by your rules."

And the country man says, "When we have an argument and we can't settle it, we kick one another in the groin, and the last man standing wins the argument."

So the city man says to himself, "I'm not going to let this farmer get the best of me. I can play this game." So he says, "Okay, we'll settle the argument that way."

The farmer says, "I'll go first."

And the city man says, "All right, go ahead." And he stands there. The farmer hauls off and kicks the guy in the groin.

The guy goes down moaning; rolls around on the ground holding himself and saying, "Ohhhh." And after about fifteen minutes he catches his breath and he stands up and takes a deep breath, and he says to the farmer, "All right, my turn."

The farmer looks at him and says, "That's all right; you win. It's your duck."

You might well say (I would, if I were in your position), "What's a supposed spiritual master doing telling a terrible story like that? I thought these spiritual masters are supposed to have their minds on higher things. Not down in the gutter."

But some of the best spiritual masters died in the gutter.

COMMENTARY

WHAT'S A SUPPOSED SPIRITUAL master doing telling *any* of these stories? you might ask.

On the other hand, if some of the best spiritual masters died in the gutter, perhaps the gutter warrants a closer look. Maybe there's more to wallowing in the gutter than we might expect.

This is one of the ways that Lee Lozowick teaches: He rolls around in the gutter until his listeners appreciate that there is more to spirituality than clean, flowing white robes and some holier-than-thou mentality —ideas that most people on the path get stuck in, at least in the beginning. While one part of the mind urges us to look good and be virtuous, another part is secretly reveling in the gutter all the time, whether we admit it or not. The common, unexamined mind is a cesspool, with no faculty to discern the true teaching from the false, and Lee is masterful at putting that in our face. At a seminar in Europe in 1998, he commented:

> Very few people have enough discrimination to tell a real master from a false master. So when I give the public teaching I assume the lowest possible level of consciousness for my audience. I know that's the opposite of what most teachers do. Most teachers assume the highest possible consciousness for their audience so that they can respect and honor their audience, but I'm exactly the opposite. I start off and I look at the audience as shit, and if the audience proves themselves to be a little more than shit, I'm very happy.—September 28, 1998, Plazac, France

With these stories—the sublime and the ridiculous both—Lee is inviting his hearers to see their own minds. And what do they see? Their hypocrisy, hopefully. Their enslavement to opinions, morality, habits, likes and dislikes, comfort and unconsciousness. Let's be honest. Who cannot find himself or herself in the angry crowd that condemned the monk, and in the fickle crowd that welcomed him back? Am I not the arrogant but naïve city slicker on a duck hunt, and am I not laughing at the guy's stupidity as if it were not my own? The teaching cannot get in if I deny my internal confusion, my darkness, my pettiness, because the teaching rests on a foundation of knowing myself, completely.

It's not that the upperworldly or heavenly realms don't exist or are not valid, but the predominant need today for those who claim to walk a spiritual path is to come down to earth, to move from conceptual idealism to present reality, whether that brings one into some temple or literally into the gutter. Temple or gutter, the teaching found there can still be sublime.

One of the aims of a tantric path is to weave together the upperworld of purity and clarity, the middleworld of ordinary everyday life, and the underworld of pain, struggle, greed, desire and failure. Lee is urging us to accept what is; to accept reality as it presents itself in every ordinary, exciting or boring moment; to accept the angelic realms and the shit . . . outside, and inside of us as well.

But, wait just a minute. Lee's joke has completely distracted me from the profound message of the first tale—*Is that so?*—a lesson in compassion and non-resistance as witnessed by a remarkable monk. Is this perhaps something Lee intended? Did the same thing happen for his audience of listeners? I wonder. Either way, don't miss it.

17

Not Saved by the Bell

There's a great Zen story about a master who was renowned for being really tough. He had a lot of students, but none of them was enlightened, yet.

In the monastery they had a big, gigantic bell. Whenever it was mealtime, each of the monks, in turn, would take this big, gigantic stick and he would hit the bell.

One day the master was standing by the bell. The monk whose turn it was to ring the bell came up and picked the stick up. But he was daydreaming, so when he went to hit the bell, it was a very weak strike. It sort of glanced off, and it didn't really make a sound.

The master got furious. He grabbed the stick and swung it as hard as he could at the bell, and he hit the disciple in the head and killed him. And then he hit the bell and went to dinner.

The rest of the monks were so struck by the master's lack of concern for the student who he killed, that they doubled their efforts, and he was soon reputed to have ten enlightened disciples.

See, those were the good old days! You could knock some disciple's head off and nobody would take you to court. Everybody just practiced harder. Try something like that now and everybody yells "Sect!" and they run and try to put you out of business.

COMMENTARY

LEE IS SPEAKING to a European audience here, obviously, as he uses the word "sect" to label a religious gathering or group. In America the word would be "Cult!" On both continents, people are nearly paranoid—or at least highly suspicious and prejudiced—about the operations of any group that doesn't fit the stereotypical Judeo-Christian models of their childhood.

Regardless of what the public-at-large would say about some apparent scandal in a spiritual community, how many students today have enough trust in their master to give him or her this kind of permission—permission to do *whatever* it takes to bring them to awakening, even at the risk of physical harm? The rarest few, I think, and Lee would probably agree.

Today, Western culture has run amuck in political correctness and a lawsuit mentality. Anything people don't like they can bring to court and receive compensation for damages done. And while we might not ascribe to this trend, we are affected by it nonetheless. This mindset is everywhere.

Certainly, discrimination is needed as one approaches a teacher or a spiritual path. Lee has frequently suggested that one look closely at the body of students surrounding any teacher as one means of making an informed decision. If the students appear dreamy-eyed and generally "holy-looking" and serious, unable to laugh at their own foibles or those of their organization, he would probably suggest that one look elsewhere. If the students by and large appear mature, different from one another, lively, generally kind, with a sense of humor; if they demonstrate basic sensibility and stability in the areas of money, food and sex; if their devotion is not flaunted, but seems genuine, their teacher's work should warrant further investigation.

"Keep your hand on your purse and your pants on," Lee once told a woman who asked him about how to decide if a particular man was her teacher or not. Seekers, in general, are a naïve lot. In the beginning it is best to go slowly.

In referring to "the good old days," Lee is making a case for radical reliance on the teacher or guru, which is one of the principles of Baul sadhana. In his advocacy for this "unfeeling" Zen master, he is asserting once again that genuine transformation is never going to result from half-hearted, politically correct gestures. Unless the disciple is "killed" he can't be liberated. By the same token, once one has decided to devote oneself to a teacher, one must give everything to that teacher. "Everything" in the sense of every doubt, form of resistance, fear, every wall of protection and every carefully guarded belief. There can be no waffling, no looking for backdoors to escape through, which will only delay the process and impede the teacher's ability to work effectively with the student. With that degree of commitment in place, the seemingly ruthless and often illogical behavior of the master will not scare one off, nor challenge or threaten the relationship to the teacher or the teaching. With the faith of the monks in the story, such behavior on the teacher's part would even inspire one into diving deeper into sadhana.

The standards Lee holds for surrender and service to one's teacher are impossible. Yet, he holds these exact standards for himself in his relationship to his guru, Yogi Ramsuratkumar. Nor will he settle for less than the impossible where his own students are concerned. Certainly, he will tolerate less, but he will never support it. But then, isn't it better to seek the impossible than to settle for the mediocre?

The nature of enlightenment and the awakened state is unbound by the conventions, ideas, projections and limitations that we ordinarily live under and expect others to live under. On one hand we know this. We read about it and study it in all the spiritual literature. Yet, when push comes to shove, we expect the spiritual master to behave in a way that corresponds to our state of being, in a manner that follows the conventions that our mind has created. If he or she whacks a student in the head, even by accident, or has sex with a student, the common reaction is to judge that he has "gone off the deep end." Can we possibly imagine that some higher purpose is being served in the student's sadhana or the master's work?

Each individual needs to develop discrimination; and each individual must be willing to pay the price for the incomprehensible treasure he or she asks for. If one's desire to realize the aim of the path is strong enough, one will see past the hypocrisy of the false masters into the authentic, if sometimes ruthless, compassion of the real ones.

18

Milarepa Redux

Lee Lozowick uses the story of Marpa and Milarepa in nearly every seminar that he teaches, and in many public talks. The classic account from Buddhist history speaks of a fierce, almost unimaginable, dedication to the teaching, and a willingness to work beyond the limits of human endurance. Undoubtedly, this is why Lee loves it. Therefore, despite the fact that two other versions have already been offered in this collection, a third one is presented now.

As a young man Milarepa left home. His father died, and his uncle basically took all his father's land, his house and belongings, and made Milarepa and his mother destitute. His mother died heartbroken and poor.

Milarepa didn't know all this, because he was traveling. But when he comes back home and he hears the story, he gets furious and says, "The people that killed my mother are going to pay." Then he goes out and becomes a black magician.

When he comes back, with his magic, he creates this big hailstorm that rains on the village and destroys all the farmer's [his uncle's] crops and kills people. And he goes, "Aaahh." He got his revenge for what they did to his mother and he feels great.

After a while his conscience starts to bother him because he feels that what he did was wrong. But he's such a great black magician that to find someone who can relieve him of his karma for his acts, that person has gotta be a very great teacher.

Milarepa asks around and eventually everybody says, "You have to go to Marpa. He's the greatest teacher of the age. He's the only one who can handle the situation."

After many adventures he eventually comes to Marpa, and Marpa proves his authority to Milarepa. So Milarepa asks for a teaching, and Marpa says, "Well, you know, I'm willing to give you the teaching but you have to prove that you're gonna be a good student. I'm not just going to give it to anybody."

So Milarepa says, "Of course."

Marpa says, "I want you to build me this house over here in the field. That will show me that you're serious."

Milarepa understands that it's reasonable that the teacher would want proof of his seriousness as a student, so he builds the house, by hand, with big heavy stones.

Marpa comes out when the house is almost done. He looks at it and he goes, "Oh, God, did I tell you to put it here?" He says, "I'm really sorry. This is the wrong place." Marpa says, "I need the house over in the other corner of the field."

Milarepa understands—okay, this is a test. Fine. He takes the whole house down and builds the house in the other corner of the field. And, of course, it takes many months. It's very hard work.

When the second house is almost done, Marpa comes out one day and looks at it.

Milarepa says, "Here you go."

And Marpa says, "Did I tell you to build a square house?"

Milarepa answers, "Yes, Master."

Marpa says, "Ohh, I must have been drunk. I don't need a square house. I need a round house."

Milarepa goes, "Okay." He takes the house down and makes a round house. And this goes on and on until he's on the eighth house.

Meanwhile, a couple of years have gone by, and Milarepa hasn't gotten any teaching yet. Nothing. All he's done is wear himself out. He's got big sores on his back. He's sunburned and he's practically starved to death from this tremendous effort of work.

Marpa is apparently unmoved. He shows no compassion—nothing.

When Marpa comes out and tells Milarepa to build the ninth house, Milarepa just goes, "This is it." He's had it. He throws down his tools and says "Forget it!"

Marpa's wife sees Milarepa running away and she runs out the back door and goes up to him. All during this time Marpa would only bring Milarepa a little gruel to eat, and Marpa's wife would sneak a little piece of meat into it or some vegetables. All the time, she was kind of the mother, caring for this poor guy. The soup of the soup of the soup of the duck . . . You know that story?

Mullah Nasruddin was just about to sit down to a dinner of delicious duck, when all of a sudden a knock came on the door. He went to the door and there were three friends.

He was bound by tradition, of course, and by being a good host, to invite them in to dinner.

They had a delicious meal and all of a sudden another knock comes on the door. He goes and there's another four or five people, and he invites them in. He runs into the kitchen and a little while later he comes out and offers them food, serving them all.

"What is this?" they ask.

"Oh, it's duck soup."

And they all have a delicious dinner and are all sitting around, having satisfied themselves.

Another knock comes on the door, and Mulla runs over, and there are five more people. He invites them in, runs into the kitchen, and a little while later he comes out and serves everybody again—soup.

Everybody's sitting around satisfied, and a little while later another knock comes on the door and he goes to the door and there's some more people. And he has them come in, and he goes into the kitchen and comes out a while later and serves everybody soup.

One of the new guests had the audacity to say, "Mullah! What is this? This tastes just like hot water."

And Mullah Nasruddin looked at him and said, "No, sir. It's the soup of the soup of the soup of the duck."

So, Milarepa is walking away and Marpa's wife comes running out the back door and she says, "Listen, I know my husband. He's right on the edge. Just one more house. Just one more."

And Milarepa says, "For Mother, okay, okay, but this is it."

He goes and he builds the final house, and then Marpa gives him the teaching. He also gives him a meditation technique and he says, "Go into the mountains and practice this until you realize the truth of it, and then when you're done, come back."

It's a very famous historical account: Milarepa goes into the mountains and there's nothing to eat by his cave except thistles, so he eats so many thistles that he actually turns green. In fact, he was called for a while "The Green Yogi," during this period.

Milarepa performs the technique and then he comes back to Marpa and Marpa gives him the next teaching, and so on.

Eventually, Marpa gives him the tantric teaching. He says, "Okay, now go out and find a consort, a partner to practice with."

Milarepa finds a partner and he practices, but he makes an error. He falls in love with his partner. So, he goes back to Marpa and he brings his partner because he's in love with her, and he wants to show her off—his great tantric consort.

Marpa sees her and he says, "Nice. I'll take her." And he takes the woman and Milarepa goes crazy.

Marpa says, "Now go practice until you have no more attachments."

And Milarepa did. At least if we can believe history.

Tantric schools are one of two kinds—either complete detachment or complete attachment. My path is the path of complete attachment.

COMMENTARY

SUCH A TALE CAN BE UTTERLY daunting, intimidating. "Well, if that's what it takes to cut through karma and get to the heart of the teaching, I'll never make it," we might say. Lee's own commentary on the matter on another occasion seems to reinforce that:

> We always use dramatic examples, but there are no Milarepas in the world today. You don't have to worry; you won't be put through that. There are no Marpas in the world today. This is the age of Kali. We're not heroes; we're like suckers. We're like running scared. The most we get to do is a little heavy sadhana—we get to confront our lives. The most we get to do—we get to "*Ram*" our beads once in a while, or get drunk, or give the guru some money and get kicked out of the ashram. Real "heavy" stuff.
>
> You don't have to worry. But we use those examples because they're just inspiring. I mean look what people have done, and they didn't even know they were going to get God. So you don't have to worry about those kinds of challenges. There aren't those kinds of teachers, and there aren't those kinds of students.

Discouraging, yes, but also enormously compassionate by virtue of its realism. Lee is urging an open-eyed assessment of one's own abilities, one's willingness to work, the times in which we live, and what it is we are attempting. Such an honest overview is essential as one moves along in sadhana. It serves, strengthens and matures us to work humbly, free of the projections and romanticism that so frequently get overlaid on the spiritual journey. A life committed to the realization of God, or truth, is not a sentimental journey for those weak of heart or resolve.

Probably no one, in this day and age, will ever ask us to build nine stone houses. But the same rigors, the same pressures on ego, on one's sense of self, and on the wish to control and preserve our private and personal lives will be asked of anyone who is serious about transformation. Demands for obedience will come from the teacher, if we have one, and humility will be learned in the School of Hard Knocks if not among one's brothers and sisters in the sangha. Regardless of there being no Milarepas today, the serious practitioner will be called upon to work and persevere, with no hope of attainment, no guarantee of enlightenment, as much as the teacher may wish it for him or her. As Richard Baker Roshi put it, "Enlightenment is an accident, and practice makes us accident-prone." Those are the best odds we are working with, like it or not.

Instead of seeing the example of Milarepa and Marpa as intimidating and impossible, or as some romantic ideal to be admired and praised but held above us, the lessons these stories contain can be applied in our own lives, even in small ways. We can use the inspiration passed down to us over generations by taking such examples as literally as possible and putting our own bodies into action, taking just one step in the direction of reliability and commitment.

Lee's inclusion of this Mulla Nasrudin yarn may seem at first like a *non sequitur*, or perhaps it is one way in which he is helping his listeners to lighten up in the midst of such a heavy narrative. But, with closer scrutiny, a lot about it relates to the themes being explored here.

We are told that, as if the ordeal of Milarepa weren't difficult enough, he is fed only the simplest gruel. In effect—the soup of the soup of the soup of the duck. Not only on the physical level, but in regards to the teaching that he is working so hard to earn, he is subsisting on the slightest whiff or faintest taste of the straight stuff. Nevertheless, he *is* receiving the essence of the teaching, albeit in homeopathic form, even if he doesn't know it.

There is lawfulness to the way in which Marpa is handling the process. When a beginning student first approaches the master it is not just that he has not earned the full teaching, but that he is unable to digest anything more than flavored hot water. His spiritual digestive system is new and weak, unable to make use of the initiations and transmissions that more senior practitioners might be able to devour and apply. The new student is much like an infant, fed light and easily digestible porridge or puree. Feed an infant a steak or cheese pizza and you would have some unhappy results. But the infant does not know this, does not know what he can digest or make use of. So, if a steak is nearby he will reach out for it and try to eat it. The new student is much the same. Not knowing what is best for him, he may greedily reach for practices he is not ready for, because he doesn't yet have a foundation or context to hold them. Only if he has committed to the apprenticeship of a master and trusts that master's guidance will this potentially costly mistake be avoided. The skillful master will not give the beginner the advanced teaching, the caviar of dharma. He will give the beginner the simple gruel, the soup of the soup of the soup of the soup of the duck. "Here, learn to digest and make use of this bowl of hot water first." When that is consumed, integrated into the student's body, it becomes clear whether or not the student can handle richer fare.

This hungering after techniques, practices, initiations as one sees in the spiritual marketplace is a characteristic of our times, and even those who may be involved in serious practice under a teacher's guidance need to guard against it. If we look at some of the great saints from various religious traditions, we will actually find men and women whose practice was simple and basic, to the point of seeming childlike. While others around them may have been doing fancy prayers, visualizations or ascetic feats, these great ones might be doing nothing but praising the name of God, or practicing the presence of God in every moment, as did Brother Lawrence, a monk in seventeenth-century France, who spent his religious life as a cook in the monastery kitchen, practicing among the pots and pans.

Another part of this famous story of Marpa and Milarepa that Lee tells in another rendering also bears on this subject of trust in the master's direction of a student's sadhana. Throughout the years of Milarepa's ordeal, Marpa's wife, Dagmema, would sneak Milarepa a small piece of meat in his porridge, or offer him a minute comfort here and there, in an effort to lighten his burden a little bit. Out of her compassion for Milarepa's suffering she felt impelled to help him in any way she could. Finally, when Milarepa was at his breaking point, unable to continue any further, Dagmema secretly brought some of Marpa's relics out to Milarepa, urging him to go to a neighboring lama to receive the initiations that Marpa was refusing to give him. Milarepa did this, and began to receive these initiations from this lama, for a short time, before Marpa discovered what had happened and informed the lama. The lama then sent Milarepa back to Marpa, who finally consented to give him the initiations he sought after. At that time, however, Marpa declared that Milarepa had been very, very close to being fully cleansed of all his obstacles and completing the inner work that he (Marpa) had set in motion in his student's life, before Dagmema's actions in rescuing him from his struggles. If Milarepa had just persisted a short time longer, even though at the point of complete breakdown and near suicide—if he had gone just a bit further—Marpa's work with him would have been complete. But the master's plan had been short-circuited by Dagmema's ill-timed pity and had to be finished in other and more extensive ways.

The story of Marpa and Milarepa can be a source of unending contemplation about the nature of true compassion.

Lee's closing statements here are particularly intriguing. As has commonly appeared in his other "trash" stories, his concluding remarks, which frequently appear as asides, are often just the turn that reveals a new door. "So," he says here, "tantric schools are one of two kinds; either complete detachment or complete attachment. My path is the path of complete attachment."

As was pointed out in a previous commentary, when Marpa takes Milarepa's consort away from him the lesson is quite clear: Milarepa is attached, identified with "his" woman. On the tantric path of detachment, one must pierce the veil of appearances, continually, and allow no karmic bonds to form to any new object, idea or person. The path of detachment is not necessarily a path of complete renunciation, however. Rather, all the distractions of the world may still be present, and in tantra they will be used for sadhana. A consort, therefore, is simply a consort—not a beloved, a lover, a sweetheart. Relationship with a consort is engaged as a means of practicing certain aspects of the teaching, and not for purposes of establishing a day-to-day living relationship with a personal companion.

But on the path of complete attachment, the consort *is* a lover, *is* a beloved, *is* a very personal part of one's sadhana. A powerful alchemy can develop in such a relationship, especially as this matures over many years together. The intimacy that arises between lovers can be an opening into seeing themselves more clearly, into a vulnerability and sensitivity to the teacher and the teaching. Ultimately, the devotion to a lover, the adoration and passion that one has for another as their beloved, can open up the channel for such devotion to and adoration of the master as the Beloved, the Divine, or Reality. Each individual can be that for another. But this is not casual or temporary. This is the path of attachment, after all. The deep bond with a lover that can develop into a bond with the Beloved requires a life-long and unwavering commitment.

Clearly the path of attachment has its traps and pitfalls, as any path does. If attachment is not complete and irrevocable, it only obstructs instead of serving one's sadhana. Attachment on ego's terms feeds only ego. Complete attachment on the teaching's terms feeds the teaching.

The elements of life and the world, the energies of power, lust, greed and competition, are also all accepted as material to work with, as potentially useful elements of sadhana. Instead of rejecting or opposing them, their energies can be harnessed, turned. A certain kind of greed or hunger for the teaching can be very valuable. These elements that we usually associate with ego can motivate us to go very far on the path, can even move us to great heights. We may be serving by rising to the needs of those around us simply out of a desire to look good or to feed our pride. But we are still serving, still helping others, and that is not invalid. Ultimately, it must be purified, and will in all eventuality, but until then such egoic motivations can be invaluable fuel. The master may even allow these motivations to remain for a very long time for just this reason, up until a certain point. On the path of attachment everything can be used to serve one's sadhana: the drives and desires of human nature, the projections onto the teacher, the passionate and personal attachment to a lover.

On the outside, this tantric relationship to life can look like any average person's relationship to life. All the distinctions that one must make and the self-observation one must bring to all things are completely invisible, completely internal. Inside, a fierce passion burns for the heart of the teaching that need never be expressed publicly, or shared with others. But to that one, *the lover is the Beloved*, and all the world is food for sadhana.

19

The Last Leap

So, a story—talking about seniority, this is from an old Hindu story.

There was a teacher that had a very large school and many students. At one point he got the feeling that he needed to slim down and get rid of dead weight. So he said to all his students, "Well, I'm going to choose a successor today. And anybody that wants to sort of be in the running can . . . let's go on an outing."

The teacher was very popular and very successful and had a big ashram and lots of money. Lots of his students, most of them, decided they wanted to be a successor, so off he went on a hike with a whole bunch of students following.

They marched up the mountain right to the edge of a big cliff. And the teacher said, "Well, whoever wants to be my successor has to jump off the cliff."

One at a time the students went up and looked over the edge, and one at a time they all kind of backed up and said, "Well, I don't think I want to be a successor."

Meanwhile, lunch was being served and they all ran to it because they were so hungry.

The kitchen boy, who hadn't heard anything that was going on, sort of came up to the front and said to the teacher, "What's going on?"

The teacher said, "Do you trust me?"

The kitchen boy says, "Sure."

And the teacher said, "Jump off the cliff."

The kitchen boy just jumped off the cliff, and landed at the bottom—broke every bone in his body. He was smashed practically beyond recognition.

Most of the students, when they saw this, decided not only did they not want to be the teacher's successor, but they didn't even want to be his students. They just thought the man was clearly insane, and they just left in a huff.

The few students that were left decided they would hang back and stick around just to see what happened. So the teacher left the cliff and walked all the way down to the bottom of the cliff and picked up this poor, broken, mashed kitchen boy, and put him in a basket and took him back to the ashram.

Once back at the ashram the teacher just moved his hands over the boy and he miraculously became healed, came back to life, and kind of looked up out of the basket . . . I was there, I know. I was one of the other students, though; I wouldn't jump off the cliff. But I was observing it.

Then the teacher gave a big lecture on trust, and so on and so forth, and understanding. And that was the story.

Well, as it comes to pass, the kitchen boy had left his can opener somewhere, so he went up to look for it and accidentally slipped off the top of the cliff and fell and got smashed up again. But this time the teacher didn't know, and that was the end of the successor.

It was a terrible, terribly sad ending.

COMMENTARY

THIS STORY WOULD JUST not work for Lee if it did not have this "terrible, terribly sad ending." It would be a little too neat, too perfect. It wouldn't challenge the reader's or listener's trust because we would know that it ends up all happy and resolved. Even though the revised ending is rather funny, it leaves things hanging in a different way. The integrity of the master is in question once again, as it was after the kitchen boy jumped off the cliff the first time. This time there is no resolve, the master doesn't, cannot, reveal his wisdom and power in making the teaching lesson. The boy dies. The end.

What? Do we still trust this master? Do we have the same feeling about him now as we did halfway through the story?

Probably not. He doesn't look so good at this point.

That seems to be the way Lee likes it. Leaving the situation unresolved, twisted from its original happy ending, creates a different effect. It's too easy to hear a traditional story with its traditional ending and think we have understood. But leaving things hanging reveals another door—a door to a deeper understanding. It forces us to wrestle a little more with the actual lesson, if we're not too busy laughing at the comical nature of the story.

If the boy dies, is the master still trustworthy? Or is he proven false? Lee is raising a tricky issue here.

Blind trust or blind following is not what is being asked for—Lee jokes that he was there, too, and he didn't jump! Yet, in any group or organization, spiritual or otherwise, blind following is common. Until one has the maturity and sense of self that only comes from years of practice and self-observation in the company of the teacher, we are all blind in some ways. Knowing this, a teacher will not likely ask a newer student, one who can't possibly have developed a rock-solid trust yet, to do something as radical as jumping off a cliff. In fact, probably no true teacher today would ever ask students to jump off a cliff for them. There are too many people whose psychological weakness of character would prompt them to do just that—as the tragedies of Jonestown or Heaven's Gate would indicate—as opposed to the rare minority who would respond from genuine and mature faith. It is far more likely that a teacher will ask one to do something that goes directly against a personal tendency, in a psychological or emotional sense. Lee is fond of telling a story of an early student of his who continually petitioned him for some heroic task. Finally Lee relented and told the young man to get himself a job and tithe a portion of his income to the community, as he was previously unemployed. The student promptly left Lee's company. That simple request was for him a cliff that he was not willing to jump off, although the consequences would only have been to his benefit.

Trusting the teacher is a paradox because, in one respect, the master cannot be trusted. Lee's constant reminder to his students is "I have no integrity." The extension of that statement is "I have no integrity to the world, to your personal lives and morals." The guru exists as one whose function it is to awaken others; to bring students from identification with the phenomenal world to living in the real world. And, as we've noted several times earlier, the principles and objectives of the enlightened state do not always encompass and respect the ideals and principles of the sleeping world of our day-to-day experience. In Western society we all want to be respected, liked, acknowledged, and treated right. But let's face it—it is purely ego and separative mind that controls these domains. Essential self is complete in itself, and does not need social recognition or approval. The teacher does not recognize these "needs" as valid, and thus is likely to ignore, offend, or avoid them.

At the bottom line, the truly compassionate teacher or master does not care about "us." He or she does not care if we are happy; if we are being recognized for our efforts; if we're receiving compensation for hard work or contributions. He only cares if we see clearly. The "us" that wants to be cared for by the teacher is the very "us" that the teacher is working to dismantle, to get us to disidentify with.

Many teachers are warm and very personal, even with people they meet for the first time. Others are distinguished by the way in which they treat all people with profound respect. This affection and respect is for the essence—the Buddha nature, or Divine—embodied in each individual, not for an individual's psychological manifestations, which may be truly unconscionable. When a student has proven their willingness to work on self, and when their trust in the teacher has matured, somewhat, the teacher may actually appear to care less and less, and pay less and less attention to that student.

While the teacher's integrity often runs contrary to the personality's idea of integrity and is therefore untrustworthy in that domain, it is absolutely trustworthy and reliable in the domain of serving the spiritual work and evolution of the teacher's students. This distinction does not come easily and quickly, however. Nor can it simply be assumed to be in place from the beginning. Over time, and with careful observing of the master, the student comes to know (more precisely to feel) that the teacher is truly in integrity with this higher principle—or not.

A teacher is not interested in students who trust blindly. A trust that is built slowly, fought for, and struggled with is of much greater value to the teacher, because it has been tried and tested. It will not falter when the master demands something that seems offensive, and it will not necessarily blindly obey either. What Lee is asking us to consider is a rare form of maturity—intelligence and common sense combined with trust and faith. The intelligence to not act rashly or out of psychological needs, and yet the trust and faith to act contrary to one's habitual tendencies. In other words, a leap for the impossible!

A teacher will not resolve for us the issue of trust in him, as the traditional story tends to do. Nor does God seem all that ready to bring the world to a happy ending in which only the good guys win. Lee's stories, too, will likely create more questions than answers. He seems committed to leaving his listeners unresolved, thick in the mystery, or even irritated. But then again, such irritation can be an invaluable source of wisdom. Just ask the grain of sand in an oyster how it grows into a pearl . . . A cliché, I know, but what else are oysters good for besides such ripe clichés (and for eating, steamed or baked, with a horseradish-cocktail sauce)?